O.C.

Undercover

An Unofficial Guide to the
Stars and Styles of *The O.C.*

O.C.
Undercover

BRITTANY KENT

Plexus, London

All rights reserved including the right of
reproduction in whole or in part in any form
Copyright © 2004 by Brittany Kent
Published by Plexus Publishing Limited
55a Clapham Common Southside
London SW4 9BX
www.plexusbooks.com
First printing 2004

British Library Cataloguing in Publication Data

Kent, Brittany.
    O.C. undercover : an unofficial guide to the stars and
    styles of The O.C.
    1. O.C. (Television program) 2. Television actors and
    actresses – United States
    I. Title
    791.4'572

ISBN 0 85965 359 5

Published by arrangement with St. Martin's Press, New York

Book design by Ellen Cipriano
Printed in Great Britain by Biddles Ltd

CONTENTS

AUTHOR'S NOTE

Immersion Therapy with Your New Best *O.C.* Bud—Me!

Know what? You and I have lots in common.

I can tell that just because you picked up this book and looked inside. If you did that, you're nosy. Not because looking in books is nosy—that's what they're there for!—but because if you picked up this *particular* book, you love *The O.C.*, and loving *The O.C.* means loving to get all up in other people's business, something that show does scarily well.

You might think it's weird to feel connected to someone based on liking the same TV show, but stick with me on this!

If you're glued to the TV every Wednesday (and couldn't care less who gets together with some reject bachelor!), then we also share a sense of humor. That's obvious! *The O.C.* is often deadly serious, like, as in almost-crying-your-eyes-out (okay, *totally*-crying-your-eyes-out) serious. But most of the time it's hilarious, with some of the biggest laugh-out-loud lines on TV and some uncomfy situations that make those "most embarrassing moments" from teenybopper magazines seem fundamentally lame. Like *The O.C.*'s Benjamin McKenzie told ET Online, "There's a lot of drama. There's also a lot of comedy. It's a fun show."

I'm also guessing that you, like *moi*, have a huge appetite for candy. Not the kind that makes you hyper and whale-like in scale—I'm talking about eye candy and ear candy. (Brain candy is not something you'll find on *The O.C.*—if you want a show with no gray cells, that's what *The King of Queens* is for!) The ear candy comes in the form of the truly amazing soundtrack piping through every ep of *The O.C.*, and the eye candy refers to the sun-soaked settings, the jealousy-inducing outfits, and the most beautiful collection of skilled actors since the cast of *Friends* first discovered caffeine.

Let's just say the cast is smokin', and not only those icky cancer sticks that show up from time to time.

If you've made it this far, we don't just have some stuff in common, we're probably intellectual Siamese twins sharing the same take on life. If that's the case, then I know you'll like my pet project, this book. As a devoted fan, I've spent my youth (okay, several months) compiling what I hope you'll agree is the ultimate, unofficial guide to *The O.C.* I dug up the dirt on the actors, cooked up a killer quiz, went on a one-girl fashion patrol, and went picture-sleuthing to bring you a package as slick as the series we both can't live without.

Now do me a favor and start flipping through my book. If you don't like it, just pretend to because I worked really hard on it and, like you, I'm a little defensive about my O.C. addiction!

Thanks for buying my book!

Brittany
XOXO

—*Brittany Kent, January 2004*

One

HOW *THE O.C.* BECAME A TV SENSATION!

RIGHT BACK WHERE WE STARTED FROM

A show as complicated as *The O.C.* does not just happen—it takes a passionate creative team, a supportive network and *a lot* of really fortunate coincidences happening at the same time.

The people behind *The O.C.* could not be better suited to the show they came together to craft. That fact begins with the show's creator, Josh Schwartz.

Rarely do we, as fans, know *anything* about the idea people who invent the TV shows we enjoy watching . . . who came up with *Gilmore Girls* again??? But there are several things about Josh Schwartz that have made him just a notch less famous than *The O.C.*'s on-screen stars. For one, Josh has been called the youngest-ever creator of a television series. Just twenty-six when the show aired (he turned twenty-seven on August 6, the day after), Josh's age goes a long way toward giving *The*

Adam and Rachel make a Josh Schwartz sandwich—he's the guy who put the "the" in *The O.C.*!
(Arun Nevader/WireImage.com)

The O.C. or Not The O.C.—
That Is the Question!

Though locals wouldn't be caught dead referring to Orange County as The O.C.—preferring instead the less formal O.C.—East Coast transplant and *The O.C.* creator Josh Schwartz missed that memo! The show's named now, but a lot of natives are restless over it. Josh has sworn to journalists that he heard students calling it The O.C.—he remembers because it made him laugh that privileged kids were trying to make Orange County sound all street!

O.C. its unmistakable credibility, especially its lifelike dialogue. Another reason the media have focused on Josh is that he's pinup-worthy himself! No doubt about it, he's a bona fide hottie.

Josh was born and raised in suburban Providence, Rhode Island, by proud parents Stephen and Honey Schwartz. He was their first child, so he received beaucoup attention from them. His two younger sibs looked up to him.

From a very early age, Josh's family noticed his desire to be involved in entertainment—that kinda made sense since his dad was a toy developer and the president of Playskool. Can you imagine all the free loot? Little Josh must've had the barn and the house and the airplane *and* the school! But Josh was more interested in plays than in playing.

Josh's dad later told the *Boston Globe* that his son's future career was decided upon by the age of eight. Josh, who attended the very exclusive Wheeler School from first through twelfth grade, was active in a number of school productions. Adoring neighbors recounted to the press that he was an easy-to-spot talent in shows like *Amadeus* and *You're a Good Man, Charlie Brown*. He was so beloved in the community that some of the local moms and daughters jokingly referred to themselves as the Joshettes. In a way, we O.C. nuts are *all* Joshettes now!

Josh combined a fascination with movies (he used to memorize his favorite ones) with a knack for writing—he began penning scripts about his circle of friends before he even hit puberty.

The most important creative decision Josh ever made was when he moved across the country upon graduation in 1995 to attend the University of Southern California's School of Cinema-Television. The school was founded by Tinseltown legends in 1929 and has a history of churning out visionary filmmakers like George Lucas and Ron Howard. Those alums are appropriate, too, because while Josh wanted to make quality movies and television, he has also always embraced the idea of creating for the masses.

While living in L.A. near Orange County, Josh observed many things that would later find their way onto *The O.C.*, namely that there were a lot of wealthy kids immersed in a superficially glamorous, sex, drugs and rock 'n' roll existence.

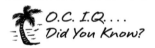 *O.C. I.Q. . . .*
Did You Know?

> The O.C. *is about Orange County, but it's shot on soundstages in Los Angeles and at beaches around Malibu, Rancho Palos Verdes, Laguna, Long Beach, Santa Monica—all within a "bubble" of L.A.—to keep costs down.*

While I assume that Josh distinguished himself by rising above the madness, he also stood out among his classmates at USC in other ways. People who attended school with him thought of him as an overachiever. This observation was proven true when he snagged the Nicholson Award in Screenwriting from USC—a coveted prize that he later had to forfeit due to the fact that he was too young to have been eligible.

Another of Josh's eyebrow-raising achievements? He sold a movie script while still only a *junior*!

In between the all-night cram sessions, real-life coming-of-age dilemmas, and taxing reading assignments that are part of normal college life, Josh managed to write a strong script called *Providence*. As the name implies, there was an element of autobiography in the project.

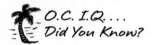

O.C. I.Q. . . .
Did You Know?

Now that the show is a success, many in Josh Schwartz's life have recognized themselves in its characters. Reportedly, Josh's dad thinks accomplished New York actor Peter Gallagher is playing a version of him. Josh himself has devilishly admitted some of his most archly-drawn characters are based on a few of his neighbors from Providence. (Not the Joshettes, I bet!)

It was "biographically based on my senior year in high school and what happens if you meet the love of your life right when life is about to begin," he told the *Boston Globe*. More specifically, the plot followed the star-crossed romance between two teens who fall for each other just before they're about to go off to separate universities. (I guess the sequel could have been called *Long-Distance Relationship!*) The script sold for $700,000 (half up front, half due if the pic was actually made) to Columbia's Tri-Star and caused a lot of envy among the other students when word got out about Josh's deal in November 1997. Okay, some people were probably happy for him, too, but it sounds better my way.

Anyway, his green-eyed peers got their revenge because while the project was kept alive for years and German director Katja von Garnier was reportedly attached to it at one time, it was ultimately shelved.

No matter—and no big surprise. In Hollywood, no movie is guaranteed to actually get made until it hits theaters. Josh persevered and continued to write, write, write, but he would suffer more disappointments before eventually striking gold.

When Josh sold a TV concept the following year, it was another insight into his autobiographical take on script writing. Around the time *Freaks and Geeks* and *Wasteland* were being hyped as big youth projects for television, Josh's take on the same genre was born.

Brookfield was an hour-long drama shot by Buena Vista International TV for ABC that followed the tumultuous life of a blue-collar kid who receives an academic full ride to a tony boarding school. It was described by some as a teen *Great Gatsby*, but with homework. (Presumably part of the homework would not have included reading *The Great Gatsby* . . . that would have been too much!) The series caused some excitement in March 1999, when it filmed in the Piedmont Triad (Greensboro/Winston-Salem/High Point) area of North Carolina near the home base of *Dawson's Creek*. And though it starred Amy Smart in a key role, it was not picked up for the 1999 season. Josh was upset—he had not only written the show, he'd also secured an executive producer credit.

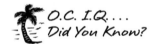

O.C. I.Q. . . .
Did You Know?

The O.C. *was the first TV series of the 2003–2004 season to air.*

Josh's next effort, in 2000, was even less successful, if that's possible! He came up with a show called *Wall to Wall Records* for which a pilot was filmed and never even aired. Ouch.

In 2001, Josh had sold a pilot to The WB and the following year came up with the idea to do a TV show based at a tabloid. He took a meeting with FOX to pitch the latter, and instead of selling them on the idea, Josh made some contacts at the network that would later come into play when *The O.C.* was being hatched.

On November 7, 2002, Variety.com broke news of a show being developed by Josh Schwartz, Joseph McGinty "McG" Nichol, and Stephanie Savage (McG's gifted partner in Wonderland Sound and Vision, who would become the show's supervising producer). Less than a year later, it would be showtime!

First, though the initially untitled show was conceived as a juicy study of social castes, Josh's co-exec producer McG came up with the idea of situating it in the Newport Beach area of his childhood.

McG is famous for directing dozens of trend-setting videos for the likes of the Offspring, Pink, and Smash Mouth as well as the hyper *Charlie's Angels* movie franchise. He was born in Kalamazoo, Michigan, but was forcibly transplanted to Newport Beach, California, as a kid thanks to the thing all kids fear—the dreaded, totally random cross-country move. And in the middle of a school year!

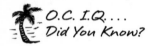

O.C. I.Q. . . .
Did You Know?

> FOX *might wind up asking for up to thirty episodes per season on* The O.C., *something they did with their previous cultural touchstones* Beverly Hills, 90210 *and* Melrose Place.

At a press junket in July 2003, McG would tell reporters, "I'm the kind of guy who graduated high school with an orange afro, neck gear, and shoe skates—so I wasn't one of the beautiful people." In this way, Josh and McG shared a culture-shock experience regarding Orange County, making it the ideal place for the series to be based.

McG was coming off the disappointing axing of his cherished cop series *Fastlane,* on which a riveting actress by the name of Mischa Barton had appeared. He'd been wowed by her and kept her in mind, a fortuitous connection.

Now that they had a premise and a locale, *The O.C.* began to fall into place quickly.

"I'm not a teen, but I'm not fifty," Josh told the *Globe.* "I remember distinctly what it was like to be sixteen . . . I want to capture that." Josh used classic American archetypes when inventing his characters, and that approach worked perfectly with the all-American Orange County backdrop.

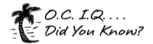

O.C. I.Q. . . .
Did You Know?

That gorgeous beach shot that precedes each ep of
The O.C. was filmed at Hermosa Beach, which is
not in Orange County.

Josh observed to the *Sioux City Journal* that Orange County "is much more of a bubble. It's much more of a heightened suburban culture."

Once he had peopled his fictional bubble with characters everyone could relate to, Josh dreamed up a never-ending series of conflicts, some of which viewers would find familiar, some of which we would find shocking—and all of which we'd be dying to watch week after week.

But if *The O.C.* is what it is thanks to Josh and McG, the show has also benefited greatly from the experience—and the experiences—of its other creative staff.

For example, pilot director and exec producer Doug Liman came to *The O.C.* from a background similar to Josh's. Like Josh, Doug was born on the East Coast (Manhattan) and attended USC. Having been making short films on his own from his toddler years on, he wound up doing a student movie called *Getting In* (1994) with Matthew Perry, Andrew McCarthy, and Christine Baranski. He went on to found Hypnotic, one of four major entities behind *The O.C.* (the other three being Wonderland Sound and Vision, Warner Bros. Television Productions, Inc., and, of course, FOX). If you've never seen Doug's movies *Swingers* (1996) and *Go* (1999), you should—they're money! In fact, *Swingers* is the movie that popularized that saying, not to mention it gave the world Vince Vaughn. (It's also one of Ben

McKenzie's all-time faves!) Doug's movies are most famous for their authentic and exhaustive sense of place—you feel he truly knows the corner of the world in which his films take place. Realism throbs throughout Doug's work, and it was his main goal with *The O.C.*, too.

😐 *"No, The O.C. isn't Shakespeare, but if this indeed is how they really do things in Orange County, then consider my bags packed."*

—*NY1.com*

"We're not going for classic soap. We're looking for the reality," he flatly told CSMonitor.com. And when asked about the likelihood of some of *The O.C.*'s plot points happening in real life, Doug would reply, "I come from a family of lawyers . . . both my father and my brother have [taken extraordinary measures] on behalf of kids like Ryan and kids who come from much worse places. It's not atypical at all for good lawyers to step out and do something quite heroic and for nobody to know about it."

😊 *"It flickers with longing and resentment, vulnerability and rejection, temptation and moral erosion. It is totally absorbing television."*

—Miami Herald

Dave Bartis and Bob DeLaurentis, other *O.C.* executive producers, don't get as much press as Josh, McG, or Doug, but even they came to the show with unique qualifications. Dave, CEO of Hypnotic, was involved with the fish-out-of-water classic *Fresh Prince of Bel-Air* and Bob had been deeply involved with place-driven shows *South Beach* and *The Big Easy*.

Casting *The O.C.* was an essential part of the final equation. After all, if actors, or even one or two actors, fail to click with viewers, shows can be stillborn. In a group effort that was as imaginative as it was inspired, one of TV history's dream casts was assembled in a relatively short period of time.

New York stage and movie actor Peter Gallagher was cast as the idealistic dad, and his presence immediately lent the show legitimacy. If Peter was on board, *The O.C.* was guaranteed not to be a mindless, California-based grope-fest. The Tony-nominated actor is known for his work onstage in the original *Grease* and in revivals like *Hair* and *Guys and Dolls,* but he's equally respected for memorable movie roles in *sex, lies and videotape* and *American Beauty.*

"What drew me to this show is I thought that there was a place for it now in America," Peter told ET Online. "I think the rich are rich[er] and the poor are poorer, and there is anxiety about the future, kids are behaving in strange ways, and a lot of 'perfect communities' are hazing. Everybody is going to be curious how the other half lives, and delighted to see that the issues aren't that foreign, and that their own experiences as humans is all you need for admission."

😞 "*The O.C. is trite, predictable and, like Orange County itself, congested . . . [It] features pretty people, beautiful locations and not much else.*"

—San Diego Union-Tribune

Peter's presence was also good news for lovelorn couch potatoes—he's definitely considered a sex symbol for grown-ups, a nod to the show's fiendish plot to snare both teens and their parents.

Further proof of that approach was the casting of forty-year-old hottie Tate Donovan, who'd just finished work on the *Mister Sterling* series and who was on the youth radar as the voice of Disney's *Hercules* and as Jennifer Aniston's most famous ex-boyfriend.

But there's good reason for guys to like the older set on *The O.C.*, too! Beauties Kelly Rowan and Melinda "Mindy" Clarke might be the youngest looking moms on TV. If they look too young to be the mothers of sixteen year olds, they are! In real life, Kelly is thirty-six and "son" Adam Brody is twenty-three, while Melinda is only thirty-one to her TV daughter Mischa's seventeen. Kelly had been in *187* with Samuel L. Jackson and is an award-winning actress and producer from Toronto. Melinda has a lengthy career that goes back to her recurring role on daytime soap *Days of Our Lives* as a teenager. The classically trained singer is also a riveting musical theater performer and the mom of a two-year-old girl.

It's hard to boil down the five young stars of *The O.C.* in such a short space, so I've given them their own full bios in this book. But suffice it to say that in choosing total unknowns like Benjamin McKenzie, Chris Carmack, and Rachel Bilson to help anchor *The O.C.*, the producers were taking a leap of faith that we now see was based on the raw talent these actors displayed in their grueling auditions. Casting Adam Brody and Mischa Barton were easier decisions to make—who's more gorgeous

The O.C.'s dream team!
(Mychal Watts/
WireImage.com)

and has a more impressive résumé than stage and film actress Mischa? And who besides rising TV star Adam Brody could effortlessly bring out the innate intelligence in dialogue, whether it be wry, emotional, conversational, or funny?

☺ *"The O.C. is refreshingly free of both Spelling-style camp and the twee earnestness that has characterized more recent teen dramas. The kids of The O.C. not only do not live in a parentless universe—they are kids who suffer for living in a heavily parented one. Grade: B+."*

—Entertainment Weekly

With everyone putting in eighteen-hour days, the pilot was filmed at Raleigh Studios in L.A. FOX was jumping for joy; the finished version had all the scale and depth that the network had envisioned, and all the glitz they knew would help it in the crowded TV marketplace. The show also had a lot of potential controversy for fans to chew on—kids were shown indulging in controlled substances and sex was treated in a very frank manner.

☺ *"Not only painless but—for audiences, I suspect— possibly addictive."*

—Calgary Sun

The *Knoxville News Sentinel* would later sniff in its review, "The teens on *The O.C.* party way too hearty for their ages, including drugs, booze and even a threesome in a hot tub."

But as McG told CSMonitor.com, "It's a more accurate portrayal of what really goes on in these communities and what these kids are really up to while the parents are away."

The show was rated TVPG-LV, to warn parents that it may be unsuitable for kids due to bad language and violence. Of course to some people, TVPG-LV means, "Watch it when your parents aren't looking—but watch it! It rocks!"

☺ *"Sexy and soapy on the outside, soft and tender on the inside,* The O.C. . . . *has something rarely seen on a 90210 offspring—namely, people we actually care about."*

—Kansas City Star

The show was formally picked up by FOX.

From the start, expectations were high. Early word was that the show was not only fun, but good.

Hard-to-impress television critic Amy Amatangelo, Zap2it. com's smart, sassy TV Gal, was breathlessly blown away by the pilot, which she reviewed in early June. "I finally had the chance to watch the pilot and I must tell you that I loved, loved, loved it!" she told her loyal surfers. "We are in need of a good, juicy soap opera and kids I think this is it. I cannot wait for you to see it."

☹ *"A weird hodgepodge of references and registers,* The O.C. *comes bearing no clear message inside its pop-soundtracked walls. . . . Its very evasiveness and irresolution makes* The O.C. *oddly compelling."*

—Village Voice

On May 15, FOX held its up-fronts in New York City, a gathering for critics to get a firsthand look at all the stars of the network's forthcoming season. The actors met the press with varying degrees of nervousness and excitement. For Ben McKenzie, it was unlike anything he'd ever experienced, and from questions he was getting, it was clear he would be cast as Hollywood's latest hot hunk when the show bowed. The high-stakes schmoozing at the after-party at Grand Central Terminal, were a stark contrast with the thank-God-the-wait-is-almost-over vibe at the show's celebratory premiere party, held July 29 at the ultra-trendy Viceroy Hotel on Ocean Avenue in Santa Monica. That night was a time for the show's sexy and overworked cast and crew to unwind and mentally recharge for the show's official premiere. I hear Adam, Rachel, and Josh were particularly energetic on the dance floor that evening!

The entire core cast and creative staff were on hand (looking foin, I might add), as were such guests as the stunning former *American Idol* contestant Ashley Hartman (who made a boo-hiss appearance as man-stealing Holly on the show), *Skin* star Olivia Wilde and *Coupling* cutie Rena Sofer.

 "Talk about your sun-kissed devil's workshop!"

—Wichita Eagle

Juicily enough, E! Online's Kristin Veitch reported in her column that she interrupted a private meeting of the minds between Sugar Ray's Mark McGrath and cheesy party girl Paris Hilton in the hotel's bathroom stall. This occurred after Paris was famously dissed by her stated crush Chris Carmack.

Informed by TVGuide.com that the hotel heirhead like *liked* him, Chris said, with his best Orange County 'tude, "She's the Hilton hotel kid, right? . . . I met her earlier tonight, and she was telling me about [her reality show]. I like girls that are cool, that can chill and have a nice conversation. She didn't have much to say. She was kinda riding the 'If he thinks I'm cute, he'll talk to me later' thing. Eh. You know, if you got somethin' to say, say it. I pick very carefully from the litter."

Some early reviews of *The O.C.* were trickling in, and there were some predictable groaners from critics unthrilled by the show's commercial aspect. Howard Rosenberg of the *Los Angeles Times* noted the show was "deep in the shallow end of L.A.," and that it offered a "comically bad . . . hour of Southern Californians as rigid as surfboards."

😊 "The knee-jerk reaction . . . would be to assume that . . . FOX is just looking for a little Beverly Hills, 90210 action to bolster ratings. But that ignores the pretty decent pedigree of the people behind The O.C., not to mention that the series is compelling on more than a few levels, able to hook both young viewers and their parents."

—San Francisco Chronicle

But many other notices reflected pleasant surprise.

"The pilot is superb," observed a shocked San Francisco Chronicle. Linda Stasi of the New York Post sounded blindsided by how much the show hooked her. "If this one doesn't last, then I give up. It's as good as TV soap gets."

😐 "The show is at its most enjoyable when it's focused on the family at the core. Anytime it strays into the world of the wealthy kids of Newport Beach in Orange County, California, it's almost painful because the characters are so detestable and yet bland."

—Knoxville News Sentinel

On August 1, ET gave viewers a peek at the show and summed it up as, "Glitz, glamour, bikinis—and deception?"

The bait was out there. Now all The O.C. needed to do was hook some fans!

When The O.C. debuted on August 5, 2003, at 9:00 P.M. following all the hype, the nets were either half empty or half full, depending on how you looked at it. Now that *The O.C.* is a certified hit with an audience that's growing, it's easy to forget that the overnight ratings for the pilot were decidedly so-so.

While notching a Top 30 debut (number 26), the show only enticed about 7.46 million viewers in its virgin outing, losing badly to the finale of NBC's *Last Comic Standing*. That was enough to build on its lead-in show, the—not to be redundant—juvenile *American Juniors*. It did deliver a 2.9 rating for adults ages eighteen to thirty-four and a 3.9 among teens, but it was hardly the smash success all the PR leading up to it seemed to have foretold. The highly underrated FOX bomb *Keen Eddie* had had a more successful first show just a few months earlier . . . and it was already resting in peace by the time *The O.C.* aired.

Was the show destined to become a future installment of *Brilliant But Cancelled*?

Not if FOX had anything to do with it—and they did! FOX had lost out when its well-liked soaper *Pasadena* got critical approval and a national Nielsen yawn in 2001, so they had some hard-

Ben and Adam became in-demand idols overnight! *(Ray Mickshaw/WireImage.com)*

Rachel makes the scene! *(Rena Durham)*

learned lessons from that ordeal. FOX rallied behind *The O.C.*, repeating that first episode Thursday, August 7 at 9:00 P.M. (it was number 80 for the week) and Monday the eleventh at 8:00 P.M. (number 69).

This strategy gave viewers more of a chance to discover *The O.C.* and also allowed FOX to test the show in a variety of time slots on a variety of nights. Even though the show had been announced to go head-to-head against *Will & Grace* on Thursdays in the fall, nothing's ever set in stone. In fact, as we all know, the show that debuted on Tuesday and was repeated Thursday and Monday is now seen on Wednesday!

☹ *"Schwartz certainly didn't waste any time selling out. The show is formulaic and pandering in laughably obvious and palpably desperate ways."*

—Washington Post

Another smart move on FOX's part was they had custom made promo spots for 182 different cities across America. So if you live in Arkansas, you might have seen the ad saying, "Orange

County, California, is 1,711 miles from Little Rock . . . but *The O.C.* is closer than you think."

The hard sell paid off. *The O.C.* became one of the season's only new shows to increase in viewership every week. By the time the fourth ep aired, it was up to 8.65 million watchers. Formerly embarrassed by *Last Comic Standing*, *The O.C.* was now kicking major A against reality shows like *Cupid* and *Dog Eat Dog*. It must've been sweet revenge for McG, whose *Fastlane* had recently hit a wall at a hundred mph thanks in part to competition from *The Bachelor*! Turns out reality bites!

Another reason the show has been picking up interest is it's been adding ancillary characters right and left, somehow using them to keep things fresh without shortchanging anyone on their Adam (or Ben . . . or Mischa . . . or . . .) fix. Alan Dale came on board as steely Grandpa Caleb, Nichole Hiltz stirred things up as slutty-but-sly Gabrielle and, most important, Samaire Armstrong popped up as Anna Stern and quickly became one side of TV's hottest love triangle.

Ben and Mischa, TV's hottest couple! *(Albert L. Ortega/ WireImage.com)*

And it turns out FOX also gets credit for having scheduled *The O.C.* after *American Juniors*. FOX is already the number one network for viewers under the age of thirty-five, and the viewership for *American Juniors* was heavily female. That meant *The O.C.* might have started with low-ish numbers, but the lion's share of people watching it were lionesses—the show's target demo.

The icing on the cake was that fans quickly realized the show's plotlines during its first summer season were particularly sun-and-sand-friendly—a red-hot idea of Josh's.

With all of these factors, success was practically guaranteed!

On Wednesday, September 10, FOX ordered more episodes of *The O.C.*, bringing the total number of commissioned shows to a full slate of twenty-two.

☺ "*The premise of* The O.C. *is somewhere between implausible and preposterous . . . But the writing is polished, the music is hip and the cast is well above average. Though everyone is good, the standouts are McKenzie and Brody, neither of whom will ever see adolescence again, but who convincingly portray a pair of likable outsiders.*"

—Milwaukee Journal Sentinel

FOX's Gale Berman beamed to the media, "*The O.C.* is, without a doubt, the big story of the summer. The success of this show has proved to be a tremendous first step towards FOX's stated goal of a year-round programming strategy. We're changing the rules, and *The O.C.*'s success has clearly proved that you can shift the paradigm and launch original series outside of the traditional September window."

So far, she's been right—big time! *The O.C.* continues to attract new viewers and to blossom into a full-fledged smash hit.

The genesis of the show is as inspiring as it is interesting—Josh Schwartz and his team have created a lasting TV legacy that gives us a lot of escapist fun and dramatic thrills, and there's no sign that the popularity of this phenomenal beach-based show will erode anytime soon.

Two

THE O.C. EPISODE BULLETIN!

WELCOME TO THE FAMILY

Just for quick ref, here are one-liners about the goings-on in the first dozen *O.C.* episodes . . .

#1 "The Pilot" (Originally aired August 5, 2003)

Guess what happens when a hot-and-hunky boy from the wrong side of the tracks (my new word for that is a *drooligan*) accepts an invite from his legal eagle to become a member of the family?

#2 "The Model Home" (Originally aired August 12, 2003)

This is the story of what happens when a bad boy tries to be good, runs away to hide out in his hostess's half-finished beach abode, and gets sucked into a brawl by candlelight!

#3 "The Gamble" (Originally aired August 19, 2003)

One of Ben McKenzie's fave episodes is this gambling-themed ep . . . and it proves it's a good bet that you should never invite your trashy mom to a boozy casino party!

#4 "The Debut" (Originally aired August 26, 2003)

Almost *nobody* wants to hit the cotillion, but someone sure gets hit *at* the cotillion!

#5 "The Outsider" (Originally aired September 2, 2003)
    This is how we do it in Long Beach—yikes!

#6 "The Girlfriend" (Originally aired September 9, 2003)
    Marissa has the most to lose (and does!) in this one, and do we really need to see Ryan tryin' Grandpa Caleb's trophy GF on for size?

#7 "The Escape" (Originally aired September 16, 2003)
    Marissa's pretty, and she's also pretty upset—so much so that she just totally wants to die . . . for real!

#8 "The New Beginning" (Originally aired October 29, 2003)
    Ryan tackles a placement exam as Marissa's sanity is put to the test.

#9 "The Heights" (Originally aired November 5, 2003)
    Doesn't the first day of school always suck?

#10 "The Perfect Couple" (Originally aired November 12, 2003)
    Are the show's pair of parents matched sets or mismatched combatants?

#11 "The Homecoming" (Originally aired November 19, 2003)
    "Get your hands offa my man" is the vibe Marissa gets when she accompanies Ryan back to Chino . . . ew!

#12 "The Secret" (Originally aired November 26, 2003)
    If you *love* love triangles this was the ep for you!

    . . . to be continued!

Three

10 SHOWS AND FLICKS WITH AN *O.C.* VIBE!
DÉJÀ VIEWS

Beverly Hills, 90210 (1990–2000)

This FOX teen-angst classic followed the extreme emotional highs and lows of a group of (initially) high schoolers intent on experiencing just about every trauma known to man. Watching transplants the Walshes navigate the circus-like social scene of BH made for highly addictive TV and made household names out of bad-girl Method actress Shannen Doherty, angel-in-devil's designer clothing Tori Spelling, too-cool Luke Perry, and eternally chipper Jason Priestley. *The O.C.* has some of this show's "youth in peril" appeal.

> ❧ *"We hope that we have* half *the success and* half *the grip on that specific audience that* 90210 *had."* ❧
>
> —McG, CSMonitor.com

The Breakfast Club (1985)

This classic John Hughes film pitted archetypal students against each other in the pressure-cooker situation of an isolated, after-hours school detention. Adam Brody's Seth is highly reminiscent of Anthony Michael Hall's Brian, the ultimate nerdy brainiac. Realism of teen life rings throughout this flick and the TV show you bought this book to read about.

∿ *"I don't think it's really 90210, and that helps me sleep at night."* ∿

—*Benjamin McKenzie*, USA Today

Dawson's Creek (1998–2003)

In this soap operatic teen drama on The WB, viewers became intrigued then hard-core addicted to the push and pull romantic and social ties between several precocious, well-spoken, middle-of-the-country teens, headed up by virginal Dawson Leery. *The O.C.*, with its emphasis on characters who are smart, young, and photogenic, definitely dives into the *Creek* from time to time. In fact, everyone I know thinks of Seth as the new Pacey and Marissa as the new Joey.

∿ *"I think it's so flattering to be compared to 90210. I grew up on it—I was addicted to it, so to be anything even close to that is an honor! Our show is a little bit more realistic in the sense that it has more—it incorporates the parents and the children more so than they did in 90210."* ∿

—*Rachel Bilson*, Bolt.com

The Ice Storm (1997)

If the movie *Go* (which just missed this list . . . see it!) is an offbeat cinematic sibling to *The O.C.*, *The Ice Storm* is their moody, chilly, fate-driven parent. One of the best American movies of the nineties, Ang Lee's intimate look at the lives of some supposedly "normal" families in Connecticut in 1973 clearly inspired Josh Schwartz in his quest to make a show where an ideal setting masks some fairly gnarly dysfunctional drop-offs.

❧ *"If anything,* The O.C. *was inspired by* The Ice Storm.*"* ❧

—*Josh Schwartz, E! Online*

Melrose Place (1992–1999)

The nighttime soap that even Jerry Seinfeld watched religiously. In a nutshell—and how appropriate is *that* word!—*Melrose Place* centered around a clique of friends, coworkers, lovers, and occasional stalkers, all of whom were in their twenties and thirties but behaved like juvenile delinquents in heat. Heather Locklear ruled the roost, and her arch portrayal informs Melinda Clarke's take on Julie Cooper. *The O.C.* owes a bit of its edgy glamour and high-stakes backstabbing to shows like FOX's *Melrose Place.*

Orange County (2002)

Tom Hanks's son stars in this light-hearted beach romp that has just enough going on to keep it from being a brain-dead teen flick. The setting and its surprise success echo in *The O.C.*

Pasadena (2001)

This warmly received FOX soaper only lasted a few weeks (sob!) but it really hooked a lot of us out there! It was all about a publishing dynasty's decline and had some absolutely juicy plots—many fans see *The O.C.* as a nice replacement for this show that was loved and lost.

Rebel Without a Cause (1955)

Okay, it's fifty years old, but . . . this movie rocks! Out of all the movies and shows listed, this is the one that most reminds me of *The O.C.*, because its central rebel (James Dean) gets into fights out of necessity and has a very soft heart. Also, his sidekick (Sal Mineo) and his love interest (Natalie Wood) could be stand-ins for Seth and Marissa. Great, classic, fun and super-sad movie to watch right away.

> ✎ *"The thing about a lot of those shows [e.g.,* **Dawson's Creek***] is that their young characters are stunningly articulate in a way that I just never bought."* ✎
>
> —*Josh Schwartz,* New York Post

Say Anything (1989)

Though not a big hit when it came out, Cameron Crowe's movie about mismatched lovers who are about to be torn asunder by the girl's college plans is full of star-crossed romance and witty dialogue. The premise closely mirrors *O.C.* creator Josh Schwartz's first screenplay and the overall feel of this movie heavily influenced *The O.C.*—inside out.

> ✎ *"The quintessential good girl always falls for the bad boy, and we really want to play that out. There are some great epic characters who have dealt with that before, like in* **Say Anything***."* ✎
>
> —*Mischa Barton, E! Online*

West Side Story (1961)

Another Natalie Wood movie . . . hmmm . . . a pattern? LOL. This movie is one of the best movie musicals of all time, flashily pitting rival gangs against one another and following the passionate love between a guy and a girl from each side. This was *Romeo and Juliet* on asphalt in the same way *The O.C.* is *Romeo and Juliet* in the sand.

star bio

BENJAMIN

MCKENZIE!

Essential Deets

Birth name: Benjamin McKenzie
  Schenkkan
Born: September 12, 1978, in
  Austin, Texas
HQ: Santa Monica, California
Height: 5'9"
Weight: 160 lbs.
Hair: Sandy brown
Eyes: Blue
Marital status: Single

Workography

TV
<u>Recurring Roles</u>
The O.C. (2003–?) "Ryan Atwood"

<u>Guest Roles</u>
The District (2002) Tim Ruskin in
  episode "Faith"
JAG (2003) P. O. Spencer in
  episode "Empty Quiver"
Abby (2003) Larry in episode
  "Abby's First Date"

FILM
None . . . yet!

THEATER
UNIVERSITY OF VIRGINIA,
CHARLOTTESVILLE, VIRGINIA
Zoo Story (?) "?"

"Hey, baby—what's *your* sign?" *(Jean-Paul Aussenard/WireImage.com)*

Homecoming (1999) Teddy
*Six Characters in Search of an
  Author* (2000) The Son
Measure for Measure (2001) Duke
  Vincentio
Getting Out (2001) Bennie
WILLIAMSTOWN THEATRE FESTIVAL,
WILLIAMSTOWN, MASSACHUSETTS
Street Scene (2001)
The Bluebird (2001)
SOHO REP, NEW YORK, NEW YORK
Life Is a Dream (2002)

MODELING
None . . . yet!

Underneath It All!

Did you know that Ben McKenzie and Adam Brody get free Calvin Klein undies? They both offhandedly told the show's stylist that they liked CK unmentionables best and the stylist rang up Calvin Klein and boxes arrived faster than you can say, "Boxers or briefs?"

Benjamin McKenzie is at once the oldest of the "youth cast" on *The O.C.* (he plays seventeen but is twenty-five . . . and a *half*!), the least experienced film actor, and the show's "breakout star." He's been compared to some of the hottest and most successful actors of the last fifty years, even though no one outside a very tight circle of friends and astute theatergoers had a clue in the world who he was just a year ago. Without him, *The O.C.* would be a totally different place—less fun to watch, less emotionally complicated, and much less visually appealing. Cinematography usually refers to landscapes, but when the camera pans over Ben I happen to think he compares favorably to a blazing Newport sunset or the crystal-blue surf pounding the beach!

Benjamin McKenzie Schenkkan was born September 12, 1978, in Austin, Texas. Everything's bigger there, but Ben (as he prefers to be called) isn't—he's barely 5'9" now, significantly shorter than his foster bro Seth, aka Adam Brody, and yet he always manages to seem larger than life when the camera's measuring his impact.

Ben has two little brothers, Nate (two years younger and a New York actor) and Zack (five years younger and undeclared at Pomona College).

Ben's dad Pete is a lawyer (not a public defender) and his mom Frances is an accomplished poet and writer. He's had lifelong creative inspiration from both his mom and his uncle on his father's side, Robert Schenkkan, an actor and the Pulitzer Prize–winning writer of *The Kentucky Cycle* and co-screenwriter of the acclaimed film *The Quiet American*. But despite these influences and the fact that his dad's parents were also actors in their youth, Ben himself was not drawn to the arts until well past childhood.

Ben describes himself as a loner growing up, more of a football buff than a thespian. In a Bolt.com chat, he confessed, "I played in Texas, which is a pretty serious football state. I wasn't anywhere near good enough to play in college, but I loved playing." Ben enjoyed being a part of Austin High's hard-to-beat Maroons and the thought of becoming a professional actor never entered his mind. In fact, Ben sheepishly admits he didn't have the guts to get up on a stage during his school years!

> ### 5 Stars Ben McKenzie Has Been Compared To!
>
> Simon Baker
> George Clooney
> Russell Crowe
> James Dean
> Steve McQueen
>
> *"It's slightly embarrassing. I'm just a kid on a TV show. I haven't done anything. I mean, it's tremendously flattering, but I mean . . . come on."*
> —Ben McKenzie, E! Online

"I didn't really hang out with the jocks," he explained to E! Online. "I did honors courses, but I didn't hang out with those kids, either. I sort of had my own group I hung with occasionally, but I've always been kind of by myself."

If he was the introverted type, he at least was not literally alone in the world—Ben's parents were always extremely supportive of their gifted son. They nurtured his curiosity about life instead of egging him on in any one direction. When he was a jock, they cheered him. As Ben would later say, they would have cheered just as loudly if he'd been an academic.

During a fan chat on the Web, Ben recently said, "I know it's a bit of a cliché, but my parents are the most influential people in my life. They supported me in whatever I wanted to do, whether it be acting or foreign service or politics or whatever it was. They were always behind me 100 percent and that was a great support to fall back on."

Ben has referred to his teen years in Austin as resembling the film *Dazed and Confused*. But he was too resourceful to fall into eternal slackerdom. Perhaps best described as a stray puppy during his high school years, Ben did have the benefit of a strong sense of tradition in his family. His father and grandfather had attended the University of Virginia, so it was a comforting sense of destiny that led him to that distinguished school. His decision to attend UVa in 1997 would lead him toward his ultimate career, though he still had no inkling of what was to come.

At UVa, Ben was a solid student with an interest in foreign policy and other aspects of politics and the government. But he never felt totally settled with this direction. His sporting background led him to become involved with a local rugby social club and he made friends around school quickly and easily. People who've met him describe him at that point as "ultra-polite" and "well-mannered," "charming," and "outgoing." He was said to always be smiling. The loner of high school was blossoming into a more gregarious guy.

Still not sure of his future, Ben contemplated joining the Peace Corps or pursuing public policy work in nearby Washington, D.C. He also seriously considered following in his father's footsteps and attending law school. He thought a lot, but the one thing he didn't think too much about wound up deciding his fate.

On what he'd later confirm was a total "whim," Ben auditioned for a play at UVa. The experience was fascinating to him—it invigorated him. If he'd been an internal kind of kid and was now a more outgoing

Ben wins hearts with that devilish smile!
(Steve Granitz/WireImage.com)

young adult, acting gave him a way to simultaneously explore the inside of a character and act it out publicly with all eyes on his highly personal performance. He was hooked and became a regular in UVa productions, earning *mostly* good reviews from his peers for roles in such challenging works as *Zoo Story, Getting Out, Homecoming*, and *Six Characters in Search of an Author*.

Even as Ben was searching for himself and beginning to find it in acting, his work in the theater was echoing that effort. The school's *Cavalier Daily* noted of *Getting Out*, "Although the search for the self is familiar to students at the University, it does not end with a diploma, and it often manifests itself in circumstances far more harrowing than simply going away to school. Marsha Norman's riveting play, *Getting Out*, explores this theme of personal transformation."

 Celeb Embarrassing Moment!

During a scene in which Ben was supposed to trip, causing a huge fire . . . something even worse happened for real! Ben really did trip (over costar Chris Carmack) and went flying through a plate of real glass. Unbelievably, he suffered no injuries and the scene was filmed as written!

As The Son in *Six Characters in Search of an Author*, Ben earned his first attention as eye candy when the school paper pegged him as "stoic and broody and quite an entertaining distraction when he isn't speaking." Ouch! But the play is about disembodied types seeking to explain themselves dramatically, something Ben was going through in a desperate way at the time. (Ironically, the *Declaration*'s December 7, 2000, review was entitled "Desperately Seeking *Six*.")

Not all of his plays were as richly self-reflexive! Ben was a standout in the Shakespeare comedy *Measure for Measure*, and was by then so high in the ranks of the department that he was interviewed for the school paper on the modernist slant of that particular production.

Our little egghead said, "In the recent past, the play has been treated one way or another, pulled in some way either by the director or with editing. I think we've stayed away from that. . . . It's very funny . . . it discusses questions with moral issues in a very modern way. It touches upon both the benefits and costs of moral absolutism."

Ben received more raves as Teddy in Harold Pinter's tortured-family classic *Homecoming,* for which he was praised by the *Cavalier Daily*. "Schenkkan imbues Teddy with an opaque stoicism."

❧ *"Once in a great while, an actor comes along whose face pins you to your seat. I'm talking about a face that you can't stop looking at because it's heartbreaking and yielding and tough and misunderstood all at once . . . His name is Benjamin McKenzie and he's so riveting, and such a good actor, that you believe that this twentysomething guy really is a troubled sixteen-year-old trailer-trash kid with a big I.Q."* ❧

—New York Post

Ben Schenkkan's triumphs on the stage at college were not overlooked by his adoring family. His uncle Pete later told the *Austin American-Statesman,* "We saw as many of his plays in college as we could, and it was clear he was very happy doing it and, in our opinion, showed great promise."

As confused as Ben had been about his direction in life, acting was leading him toward a career. He had his first professional acting gigs while in college when he successfully auditioned for some plays at the Williamstown Theatre Festival in nearby Williamstown, Massachusetts.

The Williamstown Theatre Festival (WTF) takes place in

Berkshire Hills and lasts from the middle of June until the end of August every summer. Some famous peeps who've participated in the spectacle include Gwyneth Paltrow, Anthony Edwards, Ethan Hawke, Rob Lowe, Dylan McDermott, David Schwimmer, Scott Wolf, and future *O.C.* coworker Tate Donovan.

When Ben appeared in *Street Scene* in 2001—a dated but respected play by Elmer Rice about life on the streets of New York City in the 1920s, it caused such a sensation the production was reviewed in *New York Newsday,* a sign WTF was growing. He also had a part in *The Bluebird* that same summer. These experiences cemented in Ben a determination to pursue acting in a meaningful way. Upon graduating in 2001, Ben bravely moved to Manhattan and joined the ranks of New York's unemployed actors.

In the colossally bad timing department, Ben moved to the city around the time of the 9/11 attacks. Imagine being a newly arrived transplant in a famously tough city at a time when the country was experiencing historic terrorist attacks—Ben was completely disoriented and never felt more alone.

On the practical side, he also had to deal with what quickly turned into a disastrous time for Broadway and Off-Broadway theater. With America glued to CNN and much of New York fearful of venturing into heavily populated areas, grieving, or just not in the mood to spend money on entertainment, plays were *not* the thing at the end of 2001.

Ben struggled to make a living, bussing tables and sharing a tiny apartment—he even had to sleep in a bunk bed with another starving actor.

Our hero's time in New York wasn't all bad. In fact, in 2002, he landed a role in a well-received play called *Life Is a Dream.* Ben was psyched to be a working actor in the greatest theater city in the world ("I loved the pure experience of acting on stage") and the welcoming reviews buoyed him.

Curtain Up called *Life Is a Dream* "a revelation. Virtually everything about it . . . is enough to send the most hardened theatergoer back to the library to read or reread the text by Pedro Calderon de la Barca." Ben excelled in a small role in the 1636 play about the ties that bind families (particularly fathers and sons), revenge, and politics.

Still, it was "hard professionally" living and working in New York in the shadow of 9/11, so Ben packed his bags and moved to Los Angeles, where one of the first pieces of advice he received was to join SAG and lose his surname. Supposedly, there was an actor with a similar name already listed, so Ben went with his middle name. If you ask *me*, it might just as easily have been because Benjamin McKenzie flows more trippingly from the tongue. At any rate, his real, legal name is still Benjamin Schenkkan.

> ❧ "Who knows? Maybe in five years I'll be living in a poolhouse on The O.C." ❧
>
> —Conan O'Brien

In Los Angeles, with strike issues and competition galore, Ben did not find the streets paved with gold. In the year or so he spent auditioning from the moment he arrived till the moment he got the call that he'd landed *The O.C.*, he didn't do much acting. He did get introduced to television with a gripping role on an episode of *The District,* for which he played a kid who had been sexually molested by a priest.

He would later tell *CNN Showbiz,* "I was so fed up with the audition process, where you hate yourself for wanting to get a job that you know is terrible on a sitcom that you can only imagine will get panned, if it ever gets made, and they keep telling you, 'Play it bigger! Play it bigger!'"

Pilot season is a madhouse in L.A.—it's a time when *everyone* who's got dreams of being a star makes sure they're in the city and their cellphones are on and they're trying out for every role available. Land a pilot and that puts you one step closer to landing an ongoing job on a regular series. Get picked up and you could become a self-supporting, full-time actor . . . or even a rich TV star.

Like Benjamin McKenzie.

"It wasn't quite as smooth as me just sort of being dropped off on a bus in L.A. and getting the job the next day," Ben told TVGuide.com.

When Ben read for the lead role on *The O.C.*, he didn't go in thinking he had it—in fact, he later said he'd *had* it! "I was *over* the whole situation," he told E! Online. "I had been [in Los Angeles] for a year—almost exactly—and I was just getting my feet wet in television and film. I didn't know what I was doing. I *still* don't know what I am doing. So I was just getting an agent, just trying to understand what this experience is about, the whole game."

In that frame of mind, he walked into his audition for the part of Ryan Atwood with a "sort of an *F*-you vibe." While other actors who'd come before him had been excessively butt-kissy with the producers, Ben went in like he had nothing to lose. He left with everything to gain— he so impressed them he was called back four times and continued to beat out more and more other actors for the part.

At press junkets, Josh Schwartz recalled, "We may have had sort of a different idea in mind for Ryan at first, but Ben came in and opened his mouth and we just fell out of our chairs. He already had the character, and he was so soulful . . . And finding an actor who you can just tell is smart is a really rare thing."

Ben didn't know how to

Ben looks every inch a superstar at a fan event in Hermosa Beach! *(Ray Mickshaw/WireImage.com)*

deal with actually winning a leading role on a major TV show, but fortunately he didn't have any time to consider it—they were filming the pilot about a week and a half after he was cast as Ryan Atwood.

Characteristically, Ben is humble about his good fortune to this day. He told TVGuide.com, "[The producers] have really put a lot of faith in me because you can look down my bio and, after about three seconds, you'll realize I haven't done anything. So for these guys to say, 'Listen, why don't we cast this guy in the lead of a new show?' is a tremendous leap of faith on their part, and very appreciated."

"I hit the lottery. I know how fortunate I am," he said to *CNN Showbiz.*

> ❧ *"Casting Ben was the smartest thing the producers did."* ❧
>
> —Adam Brody, ym *magazine*

When Ben landed the role of Ryan Atwood, he took it very seriously. He began working out, losing his baby fat (but not his baby face!) in a very short time. He went to Chino—Ryan's hometown—and researched the area, the way people dressed and talked. And he memorized every word in the script. No one was going to walk onto the set more prepared than the new-comer.

As he researched his character, Ben was relieved that he liked and related to the misunderstood rebel. Though they have wildly different family backgrounds (Ben has yet to go to prison), they share an outsider status, a feeling Ben knew all too well after being a Southern boy from Texas living in New York and then Los Angeles. Josh Schwartz has said that Ryan is a loner with internal struggles who's quick to get into a fight despite not wanting to fight. Ben took the role and ran with it, taking what could have been a hammy, tough-boy performance and making it into a strong-and-silent puzzle. The *Village Voice* observed of Ben that he "may be the quietest leading man on TV."

The O.C. is "like acting camp" to Ben. He told E! Online that "you just show up, and you get to do drama, comedy, romance. You get to play a wonderful, interesting character in many different ways. I don't think we're limiting him to just brooding, intense angst. We're allowing him to be funny and sharp and sensitive." The sensitivity part has captivated female viewers.

Chivalry ain't dead—it just disappeared for a while to have some work done, and it's reappeared in the form of Ryan Atwood as played by Ben McKenzie. The bad-boy element Ben is expected to project is definitely only in his character—Ryan has street smarts but Ben has sweet smarts. Sorry . . . I just had to say that.

When *The O.C.* debuted, Ben's family (especially his brothers) were thrilled that he had found a way to be successful and also be true to himself and to his art. Fans like you and me, we were just plain thrilled that something as gorgeous as Ben finally wandered in front of a TV camera and wound up in all our living rooms! Let the recognition process begin!

Ben discovers he's a teen idol on *TRL! (Theo Wargo/WireImage.com)*

"I was at Best Buy to get fax paper and they didn't have any, but this lady recognized me and went into the back for more," Ben told *Us Weekly*. But he has also expressed some trepidation about the idea of becoming a massive teen idol. "I definitely need to develop thicker skin. The speed of television means you're not always going to get what you want performance-wise," Ben told his hometown newspaper as the show's ratings escalated. "Sometimes those fears [about fame] creep into the back of your head, but then you slap yourself and think, 'Oh, woe is me! People actually like me.' What a silly thing to worry about."

But don't look for Ben on the pages of *Tigerbeat* and *Bop* anytime soon—he has officially sworn off teenybopper mags. He takes himself quite seriously. He is "wary" of teen idol status, he told *USA Today*. "If you can use the benefits to your advantage, in terms of exposure and some sort of access to do projects you're interested in, that's a wonderful thing. The other side of it, the commercial aspect of it, is interesting, but it's not exactly why I got into it."

Ben's more likely to be caught reading a book like *Fast Food Nation* (a hard-hitting junk-food exposé that he actually *has* read) than *You'll Never Eat Lunch in This Town Again*.

If Ben has had misgivings about the slant of his fame, he has been gung ho about his on-set experiences at *The O.C.*, especially his tight-knit times with the cast. The entire cast socializes frequently, including going to the movies (they usually see brainy stuff like *Matchstick Men*) or hanging out in karaoke bars. Ben and Adam have been spotted performing a somewhat coerced version of Right Said Fred's camp classic "I'm Too Sexy" for Samaire Armstrong, Rachel Bilson, and Mischa Barton's amusement.

"We come from all sorts of different places and have all these different personalities. We all get along really well—it all just clicks. They're all pretty humble and hardworking and really just fun to be around."

Considering their lovey-dovey closeness on-screen, it might be fair to ask the question: Do Ben and Mischa like each other romantically? Or *could* they? The two are officially a couple—a cute one! And the two are special friends, which is often expressed with heartless pranks on the set. The best Ben pulled was when he had the editors of the series assemble a "most embarrassing roles" tape of each of the girls from the cast, showing Mischa, Samaire, and Rachel in their worst screen performances from horror films and episodic television. Everyone found it funny, but cute or not, I hope Mischa gets him back soon!

When the show launched, the biggest question was if Ben was single or taken. He's so secretive about most things, but on this subject, he had gone on the record as being very single. He claimed to have no type looks-wise [insert stock footage of an auditorium of fat, ugly, buck-toothed girls leaping to their feet and cheering], but said he really needed a smart, funny, humble girl and someone he can connect with—I'm talking all rolled into one here, not a Hugh Hefner–style harem. He believes in love at first sight and is a self-identified "closet romantic."

But he was no womanizer as a teenager, telling *ym* magazine he "was too nervous at that point to really like girls. I still am." *Awww!* Don't be shy, boy!

Though Ben's thought to be knocking down around twenty grand an episode (and it only goes up from there, baby!), he hasn't substantially altered his life aside from taking pride in what he's doing for a living. For that boost, he's "tremendously thankful" to all the fans. And we're, of course, even more grateful that he exists to drive us crazy on TV each week.

There's no time like the present as far as Ben's concerned. He lives in a lovely new apartment in Santa

Adam and Ben *were* the teen choice at *The 2003 Teen Choice Awards*! (Albert L. Ortega/ WireImage.com)

Monica (it's gorgeous—ya gotta get out there someday!), drives a brand-new Infiniti G35, and enjoys playing basketball in a celebrity league for charity.

The future is even brighter for Ben and for Benheads like us—he is okay with the idea of *The O.C.* going on and on for many seasons (and has joked that his character will be a senior in ten real years!), but he also has plans to act in movies (like his cousin Sarah Drew, who was in *Radio*), to write (like his uncle . . . maybe *with* his uncle), and even to direct. His ultimate fantasy is to star in a Tennessee Williams show on Broadway and, you know, that is now my ultimate fantasy, too—to see him in that show, whatever it is.

∾ *"We were going to do something to his sports car, but it's his baby—if you touched his car, he'd get* very *upset!"* ∾

—*Mischa Barton, ELLEgirl*

"This whole scene is very strange. [Hollywood's] a very strange town and [it's] a very strange business, and it has a tendency to creep me out. Ryan's relationship with Orange County is very similar to my relationship with L.A.: fabulous wealth, and odd people behaving oddly, and I'm definitely a bit overwhelmed. I hope I'm hiding it well."

Oh, yeah, Ben—you *blend*. But that's the point—we don't want him to blend. We love Ben as he is, with all his small-town wholesomeness and honesty. Those traits light up the screen and make him more than just an actor, but a true star.

So far, Ben has approached his unexpected fame and glory as if it might all end tomorrow. That is a great take on life because it breeds humility and wins you friends. And what are we fans if not friends who haven't met Ben yet, but who are deeply pleased to have made his acquaintance over the airwaves?

s t a r b i o

MISCHA

BARTON!

Essential Deets

Birth name: Mischa Anne Barton
Born: January 24, 1986, in London,
   England
HQ: TriBeCa in New York City, but
   now Santa Monica, California
Height: 5'7"
Weight: 115 lbs.
Hair: Blonde-brown
Eyes: Blue-green
Marital status: Single

Workography

TV

Recurring Roles

All My Children (1994) Young
   Corvina Lang and Lily Benton
   Montgomery
The Offbeats (1996–1997) Betty
   Anne Bongo [voice]
Once and Again (2001–2002) Katie
   Singer in episodes "The Sex
   Show," "Tough Love,"
   "Gardenia," "Falling in Place,"
   "The Gay-Straight Alliance,"
   "Experience is the Teacher,"
   "Losing You," and "Chance of a
   Lifetime"
The O.C. (2003–?) Marissa "Coop"
   Cooper

She's the show's youngest cast member, but her
résumé is wow-inducing!
(Steve Granitz/WireImage.com)

Guest Roles

Fastlane (2003) Simone Collins in
   episode "Simone Says"

Telefilms

Frankie and Hazel (2000) Frankie
A Ring of Endless Light (2002)
   Victoria "Vicky" Austin

Music Videos

"Addicted" (2003) by Enrique
   Iglesias

FILM
Polio Water (1995) Diane [short subject]
New York Crossing (1996) Drummond
Lawn Dogs (1997) Devon Stockard
Pups (1999) Racquel "Rocky" Silver
Notting Hill (1999) American Starlet
The Sixth Sense (1999) Kyra Collins
Paranoid (2000) Theresa
Skipped Parts (2000) Maurey Pierce
Lost and Delirious (2001) Mary "Mouse" Bradford
Julie Johnson (2001) Lisa Johnson
Tart (2001) Grace Bailey
Octane (2003) Natasha "Nat" Wilson

THEATER
CIRCLE IN THE SQUARE THEATRE, NEW YORK, NEW YORK
Monologue (1994)

NEW YORK THEATRE WORKSHOP, NEW YORK, NEW YORK
Slavs!: (Thinking About the Longstanding Problems of Virtue and Happiness) (1994–1995) Vodya Domik

THE MITZI E. NEWHOUSE THEATER AT LINCOLN CENTER, NEW YORK, NEW YORK
Twelve Dreams (1995) Emma Hatrick

IRISH REPERTORY THEATRE, NEW YORK, NEW YORK
Where the Truth Lies (1996) Cinda

NEW YORK SHAKESPEARE FESTIVAL, JOSEPH PAPP PUBLIC THEATER, NEW YORK, NEW YORK
One Flea Spare (1997) Morse

MODELING
Ford Model
Calvin Klein Kids' Jeans (1997–1998)
Dooney & Bourke (2003)
Family Life (September 1996)
Gitano (1998–1999)
Kodak (1990s)
Ladies' Home Journal (December 1994)
Lay's (1998–1999)
Lever 2000 (1990s)
Neutrogena (2003)
Oil of Olay (1990s)
Vogue Italia (October 1997)

VOICE-OVER
Saturday Night Live (1996)
Getting Near to Baby (2001) [audio book]

With the sly, editorial wink of a classic understatement, *Venice* magazine has labeled Mischa Barton "a bit of an overachiever." She's the youngest major player on *The O.C.* (and is just about the only one playing her real age!) and yet the depth of her career so far rivals even the amazing accomplishments of stars born decades before her. She is an actress and model and—now—an icon.

"I guess I've managed to pack a lot in in a very short time without even thinking about it," she mused to *A&F Quarterly.*

She's the mesmerizing core of *The O.C.,* the girl we see as our stand-in, our role model, someone to be both jealous and protective of—we want to be like her or to *be* her, and we get an endless amount of pleasure from judging her actions and rooting for and against them.

Mischa Anne Barton was born in London, England, on January 24, 1986, to an Irish mother and a British father. She has a sister three years younger than her (her personal "heroine") and one ten years older.

If you tend to think of Mischa as a New Yorker and an American, so does she—her father was drawn to a Wall Street job in 1990, so the clan was uprooted and resituated in Manhattan. New York is the place the Bartons still consider their true home to this day, even as Mischa has had to relocate to the West Coast for her career.

As a small child, Mischa was precocious and loved attention—but in a helpful, let-me-entertain-you way, not in a bratty, look-at-me way. She adored performing almost as much as her cherished rice pudding.

As you can imagine, Mischa was just as pretty as a child as she is today. So beautiful was the future superstar that she began doing modeling gigs as early as grade school. She even appeared as a little angel on the front cover of the famous women's magazine *Ladies Home Journal* with the title "Joy to the World: Perfect Angels and Other Stories of Real-Life Miracles."

You might think modeling would add a lot of pressure to a child's life, pressure to look perfect and behave in a way not expected of other kids. But since Mischa's look was naturally beautiful (no dolled-up JonBenet poses), it was a piece of cake for the freckle-faced kid mannequin.

"I guess modeling can be difficult," she mused to *Teen Celebrity,* "but at the same time it's every[body]'s *dream.* I guess the older you get the harder it becomes."

As exciting as it was to be posing for pictures and seeing her image popping up in public, Mischa's career was about to get kicked up a notch. At the age of eight, she attended a kind of summer camp at Circle in the Square Theatre in New York along with her little sister, Hania, where she was expected to perform in front of the other attendees. Since she was taking courses there on how to write and perform monologues, she decided to do her own material. (Yes, at age *eight*!)

❧ *"I'm good at keeping secrets."* ❧

—*Mischa Barton*, Interview

She would later tell *Glamour* magazine, "I wrote my own monologue, then performed it for the parents. An agent told my parents I could be a big star."

The monologue was about the parade of indomitable turtles she would see while vacationing in the south of France with her family. These little turtles would be struggling across the road and passing motorists would inevitably stop and help them along, a sight that captivated Mischa—and indirectly led to her acting career!

She "didn't want to act. It was never like an ambition I had. It just ended up happening," she told an online magazine.

The agent who spotted Mischa was a literary agent, but nonetheless she was shortly thereafter sent out on her very first New York acting audition. She got it. And it wasn't a TV commercial or some dopey part as a precocious rugrat; it was a huge, challenging role—a central role—in an important new play by *Angels in America* auteur Tony Kushner, called *Slavs!: (Thinking About the Longstanding Problems of Virtue and Happiness)*. In this critically acclaimed work, Mischa was expected to play Vodya Domik, a Russian girl who has lived through war and suffers from radiation exposure. She would also have to deliver countless lines. While Mischa has never had trouble memorizing any amount of dialogue for a role, these lines had to be delivered in a Russian accent, something she did not know how to do at that age.

"The role required a Russian accent, but I couldn't do one," she told *Glamour* magazine. "They said I'd be *perfect* if I learned the accent, so I got an acting coach and was soon onstage with Marisa Tomei." That's right—for her first professional appearance, Mischa was starring alongside an Oscar-winning actress.

Mischa so loved working with the entire cast, especially Marisa, that the enormity of her duty never settled on her shoulders.

> *"In the role of Devon, the young Mischa Barton is breathtaking. Her performance as a girl on the cusp of adolescence perfectly captures that age's mixture of precocity and immaturity, volatile forces that are both capable of driving her and Trent to the brink of tragedy and then devising their own salvation."*
>
> —Washington Post *on* Lawn Dogs

"If I were to go back and open a play now," she would go on to tell *Zink* magazine, "I would probably be *petrified* because I would be so much more aware." As it was, she felt the experience was "beautiful" and adored the "spontaneity" of it all—even with carefully rehearsed lines, live theater is a crap shoot, and she would quickly become addicted to the unique rush of working with no safety net.

David Richard, writing in the *New York Times,* singled out the greenhorn for lavish praise.

"The most eloquent testimony in this curious, roundabout play, which opened last night at the New York Theatre Workshop, is provided by an eight-year-old [sic] girl . . . who sits, prim and patient, on a chair no bigger than she."

Gannet News Service chimed in with, "Barton, just nine years old, delivered a staggering amount of dialogue in Tony Kushner's *Slavs!* . . . She is an amazing young actress!"

Flush with the thunderous praise her Off-Broadway debut earned her, Mischa went soon after into another tough role, this time in James Lapine's *Twelve Dreams,* which was produced at the prestigious Lincoln Center for the Performing Arts. *Newsday* writer Linda Winer proclaimed, "The remarkable young actor . . . has an unearthly poise and a crisp, perfectly angelic face that makes the girl's unsentimental opportunism—a deadness beyond grief—almost unbearable."

> ❧ *"I pushed myself to try different things—stage, movies, TV—to show off my talent . . . I've been choosy with my roles, I didn't take every part I was offered—that's how I ended up with a career I'm proud of."* ❧
>
> —Mischa Barton, Glamour

Speaking of unbearable, Mischa faced the first major challenge to her composure while performing in *Twelve Dreams,* a dark work in which her character's death is foretold in a series of nightmares.

"Because it's live, some funny things can happen—like when we used live birds in *Twelve Dreams,* one of them soiled an old lady's head in the audience."

That play was still one of her favorite theatrical experiences. "I really liked *Twelve Dreams,* though . . . It was morbid, but it still had a fairy-tale–like twist."

Mischa, thanks to her good fortune at being cast in a leading role for her very first job, was always seen as a lead when it came to the theater. Her next gig—after a little-seen turn in a play called *Where the Truth Lies*—was as a street urchin opposite film star Dianne Wiest in a 1997 Shakespeare festival. It was a production of Naomi Wallace's Obie-winning play *One Flea Spare* that was staged at the Public Theater.

She drew raves all around for her latest work, which firmly established her as a tween force to be reckoned with in the world of the New York stage!

 *Celeb Crush!*

> *Mischa's rock-star crush is on Tyson Ritter of the All-American Rejects!*

The opinion of the *New York Post* typified her reception. "In the key role of the child Morse, Mischa Barton suggests the image of a marvelously self-contained cool." The *New Yorker, New York Daily News, New York Law Journal, Curtain Up,* and *Aisle Say* also considered the production to be one of the year's finest and Mischa to be a revelation.

All of this praise was thanks to her natural talent but also due in no small part to the exhausting amount of work she was willing to do toward making each performance credible and accurate.

"Theater gave me a background," she later told *Platinum* magazine. "Work, discipline, and ethics. All those rehearsals!"

All those rehearsals and not enough down time to be a kid might well have led Mischa in a new direction—she hasn't had a stage role since.

Parallel to Mischa's stage exploits, she was also indulging in an unexpected medium for someone cultivating such a respectable career path—she had joined the cast of a daytime soap! Mischa had a fab time in her lengthy engagement on *All My Children,* which afforded her a new challenge and yet a stable work environment where she could live at home and attend school. During this time she also filmed a short subject and made her first two movies, *New York Crossing* and the stunning *Lawn Dogs.*

In the former, Mischa played a New York schoolgirl—not a stretch for her, but good experience in front of a motion picture camera. But it would be *Lawn Dogs* that would herald the arrival of a major new cinematic actor.

In *Lawn Dogs,* Mischa plays a precocious girl who strikes up an odd friendship with an adult man in her neighborhood (played by future star Sam Rockwell of *Confessions of a Dangerous Mind*). The edgy drama drew excited reviews for Mischa and another chorus of surprise that one so young could be capable of carrying off such a deep role.

"Even though vital, risk-taking performances are [director] Duigan['s] trademark—think of the nasty Nicole Kidman in *Flirting*—Barton is in a class by herself in making Devon come alive in all her passion, iron will, and naïveté." So raved the *Los Angeles Times*. Reviewer James Wong called it "quite amazing," and in a three-star review, film god Roger Ebert noted that, "Barton has a lot of professional experience, but must never have

Mischa reunited with her *Lawn Dogs* co-star Sam Rockwell at a Fashion Week event in September 2003! *(Kevin Mazur/WireImage.com)*

found a role like this before. You can sense her exhilaration as she behaves the way a thirteen-year-old girl would behave—not dampened down by a conventional screenplay."

An interesting aspect of *Lawn Dogs,* one of the most compelling films of the 1990s, is that Mischa's character lives in a gated community—a concept she'd encounter with another character a few years later . . . on *The O.C.*!

"*Lawn Dogs* . . . gave me the first taste of publicity and traveling," Mischa told *Platinum.* "I was only eleven. I knew after that it was what I wanted to do."

At year's end, *Lawn Dogs* was named the best film of 1998 by Michael O'Sullivan in the *Washington Post,* and it was clear that Mischa Barton was considered one of the best child actors of the decade.

Mischa was energized by the making of *Lawn Dogs* and became curious about the moviemaking process. She began to ask questions and investigate the processes swirling around her when she signed on for her film *Pups,* which would be yet another nervy adolescent role.

"When I'm filming, I'm enthusiastic, because I care so much about the work, I'm hardly ever in my trailer. When I'm not acting in a scene, I go on the set and sit with the director. I've learned a lot about filming by watching how things work," she told *Glamour.*

Pups, which was branded "stellar" by *Time Out New York,* was an indie film with an unfortunate sense of timing. The role of a thirteen-year-old gun-toting bank robber was juicy, but it came out two days before the Columbine massacre, making it an uncomfortable film for most people in those harrowing days. Why pay money to go see a movie about kids with guns when it was an image you couldn't escape on TV at the time?

Mischa was growing up. She got her period at thirteen during the making of *Pups* (hey, she told *Shout!* this tidbit in 2001 so don't shoot the messenger!) and she began to experience all the normal push-and-pull feelings of adolescence. Except in Mischa's case, she was—despite starring as so many troubled teens—relatively angst-free.

"I grew up through all my characters," she observed to *Shout!* "so anything awkward I've experienced in real life, my characters have experienced, and more!"

Not every piece that Mischa was involved with as a younger actress was as moody as *Pups*. In fact, she had a brief role in the Hugh Grant–Julia Roberts romantic comedy classic *Notting Hill*. And yes, she *adored* Hugh! "He was really nice and he was even born in the same hospital as I was in Nottingham, England!"

Released in May 1999, *Notting Hill* would go on to make over $116 million at the American box office.

Her next part would be another small role in a big commercial movie—so big, she will be lucky to *ever* appear in another film that matches it at the box office.

Mischa Barton had a sixth sense about *The Sixth Sense*. She just *knew* it was going to be a special film, one that would go over well with audiences. In it, she plays the late Kyra Collins, a dead girl, in one of the film's most strikingly haunting sequences. As the movie snowballed into a three hundred-million-dollar hit, audiences left screenings captivated by Mischa's role—and grossed out by her graphic vomiting scene!

The "vomit" was actually a mixture of breakfast cereal that she would hold in her mouth and spit up, something that was none too pleasant to begin with, let alone when you add in that all the sets she was on were refrigerated to make her breath visible and call to mind the chill of purgatory. She spent an hour and a half having her dead-girl makeup applied and found the entire role so overwhelming it left her in tears every day.

But she told *Paper* magazine, "I don't mind emotionally draining roles; I think they're kinda fun."

Up until the release of *The Sixth Sense*, Mischa had managed to keep her acting career off the radar of most of her childhood friends. But do you know *anyone* who hasn't seen *The Sixth Sense*? Me, either!

She told *Interview* magazine, "One of my friends said, 'You didn't tell me you were in the movie! I was so scared I ran out of the theater! You were dead! My friend was dead!'"

After doing good work in a mystery film called *Paranoid* with a young Jessica Alba, Mischa landed a risqué role as a fourteen-year-old virgin who hopes *not* to be one for much longer in *Skipped Parts*. This 2000 film costarred Brad Renfro, Drew Barrymore, and Jennifer Jason Leigh, with whom Mischa worked closely and bonded.

> **Dream Casting!**
>
> Mischa has said she'd most love to work with Jodie Foster or Ben Kingsley . . . and that she dreams of playing a queen in a period piece!

"Working with Jennifer . . . was wonderful. She was very nice and we got along well. I was also impressed by how mature and prepared she was on the set."

The new buddies would hang out at Jennifer's home, where they even watched a series of movies together—including the older actress's own thriller *Single White Female*!

Titled *The Wonder of Sex* in Europe, *Skipped Parts* was distinguished enough as a film that it debuted at the Cannes Film Festival. That led to a Barton family trip, one that gave Mischa fond memories of seeing her little sister on the beach of the French Riviera. The film's director was Tamra Davis, and the splash the film created led to Tamra getting the thankless job of directing Britney Spears in (the pretty dreadful, IMHO) *Crossroads*.

On Zap2it.com, Mischa admitted of *Skipped Parts*, "I wanted to do that role . . . because I like to keep my roles varied a lot, and it was set in the sixties, and I thought that was a visually interesting time."

She was cast but did not appear in Kevin Costner's *Dragonfly*, but she did have fun as a ballerina in the Showtime Family Movie *Frankie and Hazel*, which costarred the legendary Dame Joan Plowright and which was financed by Barbra Streisand's Barwood Films.

"I do intelligent roles," she said at the time. "I don't want to be labeled as doing silly movies. I'm more mature than kids my age because I'm constantly surrounded by adults."

Her next film demonstrated this beautifully.

Mischa's performance as Mary "Mouse" Bradford in *Lost and Delirious,* more than any other role, is probably most fondly remembered by her diehard fans. It's not a movie that had the global reach of *The Sixth Sense,* but is instead a cult classic, a highly regarded and quite racy film about boarding-school girls discovering sexuality's pleasures and pitfalls. Mischa's character in this film adaptation of the Susan Swan novel *The Wives of Bath* is the youngest of three roommates, and the two other girls (Piper Perabo and Jessica Paré) are secret lovers. In this English-language debut by respected Swiss director Léa Pool, something most filmgoers who saw it fixate on is its stylized and erotic use of sex scenes (not involving Mischa). But while it only grossed about $300,000 at the box office when it was released in July 2001, it *engrossed* many critics, winning three Canadian Oscars. This movie and her next—*Julie Johnson*—debuted at the Sundance Film Festival.

Two things stood out in Mischa's memory about making *Lost and Delirious.* One was that her director didn't have a strong grasp on the English language, so when she tried to communicate with the cast, instead of being very vague, she would go to such lengths to make herself clear that the instructions were invariably even more lucid than if they'd been spoken by an American. The other was not so nice—for a scene demanding attentive hawks, Mischa had to keep dead chicks in her pockets for their lunch. *Yum!*

Roger Ebert, who had been so taken by Mischa in *Lawn Dogs,* continued his love affair with her screen work when he published "Roger Ebert's Thoughts on *Lost and Delirious*" ahead of its release after discovering it at Sundance.

Sounding like a lovesick sailor gazing upon a picture of a buddy's girlfriend, he wrote that he was "absorbed from beginning to end because the characters are enormously interesting and likable. And because they are gorgeous. And because you could hear a pin drop in the 1,400-seat Eccles Center during the sex scenes, which are not explicit, but are erotic."

Proving her versatility and the ease with which she could go from lesbian art house steamy to Disney Channel chlorinated splashy, Mischa signed on to be the love interest of hunky Ryan Merriman in the telefilm *A Ring of Endless Light,* an inspirational dolphin movie that enjoyed high ratings over many, many reairings.

"She ends up with . . . the dolphin boy," Mischa told Zap2it.com. "She hated the other one, who had a Ferrari, and she ends up with the dolphin one. Although on set, I was leaning toward the Ferrari!"

She loved working in the water with dolphins and very much enjoyed the beauty of Australia, where the movie was made. It was a bit scary having to hold her breath underwater while dolphins fought for fish above her, but she did eventually grow quite comfortable with the eerily intelligent animals.

A Ring of Endless Light, based on a Madeleine L'Engle novel, won Disney Channel a Humanitas Prize for Children's Live Action. The cash award is for "writers whose produced scripts communicate values that enrich the human person."

Flip-flopping from indie movies to the mainstream had become second nature to Mischa, who told *Seventeen* in 2002, "I don't really have a preference. I just want to play a good character. The only problem with independents is that you can have an amazing role in an amazing movie, but not many people see it."

Such was the case with both *Julie Johnson* (with the ill-fated Courtney Love and *Six Feet Under*'s Lili Taylor) and *Tart,* in which Mischa and Dominique Swain got to vamp it up as bored, rich, Upper East Side New York schoolgirls. Both movies came and went (or in *Julie Johnson*'s case, never arrived at all!) without much ado, representing an artistic and commercial lull for Mischa, and yet a continuation of her penchant for offbeat roles. *Tart,* set in the 1980s and focusing on drugs, was a movie she chose to do in order to hone her "fun" British accent skills.

But TV had been good to Mischa as a soap star and then with Disney, so she stuck with a Mouse affiliate and signed on to play Katie Singer for ten episodes of the ABC drama *Once and Again.* It was also a return to a lesbian-themed role, as Evan Rachel Wood's character on the ratings-challenged show was confused about her sexuality and shared a televised kiss with Mischa's character. The unprecedented smooch was in the show's most watched era, but it never lived up to ABC's expectations, and *Once and Again* got the big kiss-off.

Mischa left public school thanks to pushy teachers who wanted her to quit acting. She told *ELLEgirl* magazine that to those smarty-pants she now says, "I hope you're watching my show!" Even in private school, Mischa was maintaining a relatively normal school life for part of her childhood and into her teen years, attending a middle school on the Upper East Side of Manhattan and supplementing that with online studies through Laurel Springs, a California-based Web program.

She was doing better than ever in her public life, too, having just been voted Least Annoying Actress of the Year for 2002. A dubious honor, but in this day and age of overexposure, celeb shenanigans, and a mounting resentment by the moviegoing public of the people who entertain us onscreen, an honor nonetheless.

She told *Teen Vogue* her big challenge for the year had been working on getting her driver's license, but when she played the rebellious Simone on an episode of the McG-created TV series *Fastlane,* her career kicked into high gear. This fortuitous collaboration led to an acquaintance with McG, that in turn led to Mischa trying out—way after early-bird Peter Gallagher and just before last-second arrival Ben McKenzie—for McG's next project, a soaper called *The O.C.*

Normally, Mischa has taken roles in which her looks are not played up. In fact, she often looks totally different from her normal self and considers it a compliment when people can't recognize her from her many screen roles.

"You don't have to have a pretty face to be an actress," she told *Seventeen.* "I like to do roles where I'm supposed to be ugly or weird or punky—not just another pretty face."

But for *The O.C.,* Mischa faced an audition for a starring, glamorous role of the kind she'd never had before. She has confessed to being nervous at auditions—to think she was probably more uptight trying out for a straightforward role than she ever had been for any of her earlier out-there roles is quite funny!

For *Venice* magazine, Mischa recounted her *O.C.* audition: "I went in to meet with McG and Josh Schwartz and we were talking about the character and where they wanted to go with it. I loved the pilot; I was just attracted to Marissa because it was clear in the pilot that she was the one out of the more superficial set who had a greater depth to her. And she was aware that she was privileged and she knew that she was living a good life and that it might not always last. And I was like, 'That could really, if you develop it right, be such an incredible character.'"

Schwartz saw her as a young Audrey Hepburn and *had* to have her for the part—she got it!

Within days, she was reading with "lots of boys" to help out in the casting of Ryan Atwood, a part that would of course go to Ben McKenzie.

As she read more of the material, she became firmly convinced that *The O.C.* wouldn't become one of those silly shows that she might be embarrassed to have taken somewhere down the line.

"It really connects with people," she told *Us Weekly*. "There's a lot of gritty stuff in there . . . But that's what teenagers experience, and we want to keep it as real as possible."

She was adamant during an interview with *Women's Wear Daily* when the topic of the show's more lurid parties and violent sprees came up. "We actually show a good spectrum of how kids party . . . It's not all glamour."

Her on-set experiences with the cast of *The O.C.* have been a joy for Mischa, who never takes herself too seriously while working and is known to be "on" and engaging at all times. She is the ultimate nice girl—and if anyone has earned the right to be a bit of a diva, it's her.

"I've had fellow actors tell me, 'You have to throw more tantrums!'" she laughed to *Entertainment Weekly*. But the tantrums never come with Mischa Barton. Don't look for a Shannen Doherty ending to her *E! True Hollywood Story*.

Ben McKenzie has ratted her out as a bit of a klutz on the set, and he's teased her mercilessly for her habit of bumping into things, tripping, and even falling to the floor. Hardly the "perfect girl" (*Seventeen*), "big thing" (*Glamour*), "It girl" (*Entertainment Weekly*), and "sexy" champ (TVGuide.com, which had pitted her against Kate Bosworth) that the hype machine has created, Mischa is truly a normal girl with abnormal talent, an ethereal presence combined with an infectious mirth.

As part of her newfound household-name status, and as befits her come-on-ya-gotta-admit amazing beauty, Mischa has returned to her modeling roots. She posed for Calvin Klein at eleven, but at seventeen she is the Neutrogena SkinClearing makeup girl in print and on TV. She's also endorsed Dooney & Bourke bags.

> ✎ "It's one of those things I can't stop doing because I love doing it . . . It's where my passion lies." ✎
>
> —*Mischa Barton on acting*, A&F Quarterly

And like every ingénue—except maybe Marissa Jaret Winokur—Mischa was accused of being dangerously thin in an October 12, 2003, article in the 'bloid *In Touch*. She's not too thin. There is such a thing as too thin, but Mischa has been the same proportionate size her whole life. She's got the genes, so get used to it and pass the Doritos!

She's quickly become a must-have for events like the VH1/Vogue Fashion Awards and other ceremonies and benefits, and her style choices could fill a book of their own, they're so confident and so uniformly flattering and smart. She's been recognized on the street, in her car, and even by gushing skinheads at a Sex Pistols concert.

Mischa has also managed to avoid believing her own hype, sticking to her morals and her serious outlook and eschewing the craziness associated with the lifestyles of former costars like

Courtney Love, Brad Renfro, and Bijou Phillips—of whom she told *A&F Quarterly,* "They act the way people say they do . . . there's a reason they have those reputations."

Currently living in Santa Monica with her mom and little sis Hania, Mischa is enjoying the good life. She's playing a character whose development trajectory will bring her closer into line with who Mischa is herself (that's Josh Schwartz's plan for most of the characters on the show). She's got down time to read cherished classics like *The Grapes of Wrath* in Santa Monica's trendy cafés now that she graduated high school from New York's Professional Children's School, situated next to Lincoln Center. (She'd technically graduated early—at fifteen—but had opted to continue with her studies.)

"I'm really lucky to be able to separate my life between New York and L.A.," she raved to *Zink.* "It's the best situation to be able to have my friends, apartment and normal life in the city, and then spend the rest of my time traveling and working in L.A. These days, I pretty much split my time equally between New York and L.A., and it's that balance that keeps me sane. In New York, it's really difficult for people to recognize you because it's such a bustling city."

Asked by *Movieline*

Mischa is today's biggest teen fashion plate and one of her generation's biggest stars! *(Theo Wargo/WireImage.com)*

to tick off her fave things about L.A., Mischa offered that they would be "things we don't get in New York—sitting out in a café in beautiful weather or going to the beach or amusement parks because we don't get to do those things. We're city kids. I play baseball, basketball, soccer, I swim, I learned to surf. When I'm in L.A., I go Boogie boarding and surfing. I really like Manhattan Beach. They have a cute little community."

A typical day for Mischa, assuming it's not one of those hellish all-day shoots for *The O.C.,* would be a photo shoot for a magazine, an event, and attending a celebrity's birthday bash (she was one of the guests at former coworker Shane West's).

What's next for Mischa? She's got an occult thriller called *Octane* that's been loitering about, waiting for release—a movie she shot in Luxembourg and England—and she is dating co-star Ben McKenzie.

Mischa told *Spin* that she thinks her character Marissa will gravitate toward her own taste in guys, "meaning that, of the two guys, she'll definitely be attracted to the bad boy." And she announced to Jimmy Kimmel (during her late-night talk show debut) that she was dateless, having given up her last boyfriend when she had to move from New York to film *The O.C.* That was pre-Ben!

She's been so busy with her work as a seventeen year old that you might be thinking the same thing I am: How can she just settle down on *The O.C.,* and does this mean she might— gulp!—leave the show soon?

She told the cool online 'zine *Green Room* of the steady stream of new offers coming her way that she tries "not to become too involved in it. I don't run out on everything I see because I like to be more selective about the kind of scripts or roles I want to do. My mother or management will read the scripts first and then I'll look at them."

Not exactly the words of the next Suzanne Somers, David Caruso, or Rob Lowe—all famous actors who've left shows at the height of their popularity for one reason (money) or another (money).

So sit back and relax—as fans of *The O.C.,* we're lucky to

have someone as brainy and talented and beautiful as Mischa Barton. She appears set to stick with the show for the long haul, and I believe she will wind up a top movie actress as well as a TV star. From her work that I've seen, there's nothing Mischa can't do—and very little she hasn't tried! She recently starred as the female love interest in Enrique Iglesias's "Addicted" music video, and I've got to admit that I'm totally hooked on Mischa Barton!

star bio

ADAM

BRODY!

Essential Deets

Birth name: Adam Brody
Born: April 8, 1980, in San Diego,
   California
HQ: Santa Monica, California
Height: 5'11"
Weight: 160 lbs.
Hair: Dark brown
Eyes: Green (with brown contacts)
Marital status: Single . . . but
   dating Emily Montague

Workography

TV
Recurring Roles
Undressed (2000) Lucas in
   episodes #316–#323
Once and Again (2000–2001)
   Coop in episodes "Cat-in-Hat,"
   "I Can't Stand Up (for Falling
   Down)," and "Busted"
MTV's Now What? (2002) Zack
   Altman [originally titled *The
   Sausage Factory* and aired in
   non-U.S. markets in 2001]
Gilmore Girls (2002–2003) Dave
   Rygalski in episodes
   "Application Anxiety," "One's
   Got Class and the Other One
   Dyes," "They Shoot Gilmores,

Oh, Adam! *(Steve Granitz/WireImage.com)*

Don't They?," "A Deep Fried
Korean Thanksgiving," "Lorelai
Out of Water," "Swan Song,"
"Face-Off," "Keg! Max!," and
"Say Goodnight, Gracie"
The O.C. (2003–?) Seth Cohen

Guest Roles
The Young and the Restless (1999)
City Guys (2000) Customer #1 in
   episode "Makin' Up Is Hard to
   Do"
Other People (2001)
Grounded for Life (2001) Brian in
   episode "Action Mountain High"

Judging Amy (2001) Barry "Romeo" Gilmore in episode "Romeo and Juliet Must Die—Well, Maybe Just Juliet"

Go Fish (2001) Billy in episode "Go Student Council"

Family Law (2001) Noel Johnson in episode "My Brother's Keeper"

The Andy Dick Show (2002) Buyer at Nikka Costa Show

Smallville (2002) Justin Gaines in episode "Crush"

Telefilms

Growing Up Brady (2000) Barry Williams

Music Videos

"Too Bad About Your Girl" (2003) by the Donnas

FILM

Never Land (2000) Jack

The Silencing (2000) Karl

Roadside Assistance (2001) Rusty

American Pie 2 (2001) High School Guy

According to Spencer [aka *Garage Sale*] (2001) Tommy

The Ring (2002) Kellen, Teen #3

Grind (2003) Dustin Knight

Missing Brendan (2003) Patrick Calden

THEATER

None . . . yet!

MODELING

None . . . yet!

When *USA Today* puts you in that little box in the upper-right corner of its front section, that's usually a hands-down "Score!" for any actor. For Adam Brody, the twist was that his was the face being used to sell an article entitled "Geek Chic." Add the fact that hard-news giant *Newsweek* dubbed him "adorkable," and there is definitely a slight trend going on here.

But Adam's having the last laugh. While his character Seth was originally conceived as the nerd on *The O.C.*, Adam was recently voted as the hottest, sexiest dude on the show by 50 percent of the readers of *J-14* magazine—there's nothing square about *that*. It's also a good indication that—as he himself would argue—the real Adam Brody is slowly but surely infiltrating the Josh Schwartz creation known as Seth Cohen.

Adam's life story is anything but dweeby.

Adam was born April 8, 1980, in San Diego, California. His mom Valerie is a creative sales manager (and graphic artist) and his dad Mark provides legal counsel and works as a risk manager at Alliant International University, an institution devoted to diversity and "learning without boundaries."

Adam's 10 Fave Things: A Checklist

> Vince Vaughn—Ironic that he so worships the actor made famous by *Swingers,* a movie that made Doug Liman famous, who in turn helped make Adam famous on *The O.C.*!

> Comic actors like Ben Stiller and Owen Wilson—Adam's punchy delivery would work well in a film with either or *both* of these comic geniuses!

> *X-Men*—Adam is an unapologetic comic-book geek.

> Emo music—The thinking kid's punk rock.

> Death Cab for Cutie—The band has so blown Adam away that his fandom was picked up by Josh Schwartz, who ensured their work would appear on *The O.C.*!

> Naomi Watts—Um, of course!

> *Kelly Slater Pro Surfer*—A game about surfing is sort of like a picture of a good time . . . why not just *do* it? But Adam surfs real-time as well.

> Reading the newspaper—He's an informed kinda guy.

> Politics—Adam is interested in the current political climate, a trait he shares with both Mischa Barton and Benjamin McKenzie.

> *Everything Is Illuminated* by Jonathan Safran Foer—This out-there (I'm talking *way* out-there) mind-game of a novel about the lingering effects of the Holocaust was one of 2003's buzz books. Adam is human buzz. Hence, he liked this read!

Rounding out the Brody Bunch (this name will take on new meaning as you read about Adam's early TV credits later) are his brothers, fraternal twins (and major hotties) Matt and Sean.

They lived in a tight-knit community not unlike Newport Beach, but nowhere near as swanky. And as far as we know Adam wasn't beaten up regularly at wild parties. He did attend local block parties for several years, if that counts.

Adam has always been extremely responsive to a variety of music, particularly emo—short for *emotional* and used loosely to describe a huge array of punk-sounding music. Emo is big in

Cali, and Adam's taste for that sound would later infect the soundtrack of *The O.C.*

Adam was not one of those kids who had it in his mind that he just *had* to act. In fact, he never participated in school plays or did any acting until the end of his teens. Instead, he was a classic bleached-blond surfer dude—he even once worked at Mother Board Shop in La Jolla. That wasn't his only job, though.

Adam also worked for a long time at the La Jolla Blockbuster franchise, where he had a steady stream of free movies. He told the *San Diego Union-Tribune* the job was "incredibly boring," but the exposure to films good, bad, and ugly did get his creative juices flowing (remember, Quentin Tarantino acquired his film expertise as a vid clerk, too!). Still, it wasn't until after he'd graduated from Scripps Ranch High School in 1998 and was taking courses at MiraCosta College of Oceanside that he considered exploring acting.

Adam's lack of direction was a major bone of contention in his family—this might sound familiar to some of you.

"In high school, I had a tough relationship with my dad," Adam told *Entertainment Weekly*. "Now I look back and I don't know why I was so mean. He was right every time. It's hard because I think, 'Why is Seth turning his back on his dad?'"

According to Adam's interview with *ELLEgirl,* he was "a true surfer and skater boy, but it never occurred to me to try and go pro because at fifteen the really talented guys were already well on their way."

A bit aimless but plenty eager to become independent, Adam hatched a scheme. While he was bobbing in the waves on his surfboard one time, he dreamily came up with a plan: since he and his best buddy, Ari Davis, had no jobs, goals, or even relationships tying them down, why not do the Hollywood thang and move there to seek movie and TV parts?

"I hadn't acted in high school. I just grew up surfing and stuff . . . I was not into school, there wasn't anything I wanted to do. The only thing in my career counseling class that looked at all interesting was acting. I was kind of drifting. I thought maybe I'd own a surf shop."

The duo made the move to L.A. in January 1999, but not without a plan. First, Adam hired an acting instructor; he wasn't so cocky as to think he would get hired just because he was a nice guy who needed the work. He knew he needed to practice at the craft.

"I made a deal with myself," he would tell the *Tribune* once his career was on the rise. "I would . . . give myself one year, try acting my absolute hardest." That meant he would sacrifice part-time jobs (like stints at French Connection, Mr. Damiano's Pizza, and the Beverly Hills Hotel) if a tempting audition came up. That also meant if he failed to get any parts that year, he'd move back home. Ari didn't last in L.A., but Adam—fortunately for us all—did.

While living in Santa Monica, Adam shared a horrifyingly tiny room, the kind of thing struggling actors do all the time.

"The room was L-shaped," he told his hometown paper, as if still shell-shocked, "and we had bunk beds in one end. It was so small, only one person could be vertical at a time. We had to take turns eating because one person would have to be lying down on the bed. It wasn't much bigger than a cell at juvenile hall."

His first auditions were nothing to write home about, either. "You find yourself at auditions screaming at a fake dinosaur who wants to take your Twix bar."

During this time, Adam held down a job at the Robinsons-May store on the tourist-congested Third Street Promenade near the Pier. Despite his busy schedule, he began to formulate a theory: If he truly applied himself to acting, got an agent, went on every audition, and never goofed off with a part, he would eventually succeed. He convinced himself that if he simply made himself known, fame would come to him.

It wasn't fame that came, at least not initially—it was seven lines on *The Young and the Restless*. Young and restless, Adam was happy for the exposure and the (small, but . . .) pay.

Adam was about to embark on a never-ending series of small

roles on TV shows like *Undressed* and *City Guys,* but his first huge break was when he was cast to play Barry Williams, aka Greg Brady, in *Growing Up Brady,* a fairly cheesy biopic on the series and its highs and lows. It may seem like an eye-roller now, but that kind of gig is golden for newbies. It paid so well that Adam quit his day job(s) and has been a full-time professional actor ever since.

On the down side, Adam—unlike, for example, a hot starter like Mischa Barton—had to deal with some dumpy reviews early on instead of the encouraging (or at least polite) ones actors hope for.

A source no less authoritative than *Variety* stated about *Growing Up Brady,* "Charmless acting, by-the-numbers direct-ing, and a seemingly dashed-together script make for a thor-oughly un-*Brady* experience. NBC has been using a clip of Marcia (Kaley Cuoco) slowly stepping into a pool to seduce Williams (Adam Brody), a story told from a distinctly different perspective in Williams's book of the same name." But *Variety* did go on to note that, "Brody has some of the goofball charm of Greg's early years," and hey—he got to share screen time with the lovely and talented Kaley Cuoco . . . *Kaley! Kaley! Kaley!* (Sorry, my *Brady* fetish is showing.)

Soon, a trifecta of memorable TV roles would come Adam's way, giving him the experience, confidence, and fan recognition that would propel him to the next level, and take him from Santa Monica to Newport Beach.

Adam had been adorable on the very daring *Undressed* series for MTV, but he was just plain hilarious on the underappreci-ated cult series *MTV's Now What?*, originally entitled *The Sausage Factory.* Adam's comic timing was brilliant on the show, which had (and even though it's in TV heaven, *still* has) diehard fans devoted to its every line.

He also had a great guest shot on The WB's *Smallville* as a vengeful art student with telekinetic powers.

But the role that truly put Adam directly in the spotlight and virtually guaranteed he'd go on to much bigger things was his en-dearing turn as Dave on *Gilmore Girls.* The show, one of TV's best written and most beloved, offered Adam lots of screen time over an arc of episodes. The rapid-fire dialogue perfectly suited his own manner of speaking and cracking wise. This showcase job directly led to Adam's casting on *The O.C.*—who *couldn't* see he was a series star trapped in the role of a recurring guest star?

Speaking with EW.com, Adam said, "The truth is, us nonfamous kids have to go out and audition. Pilot season for someone who auditions is about going out for as many things as you can and seeing what sticks. Thankfully, I got stuck to something good, 'cause there's plenty of bad ones."

When Adam landed *The O.C.,* he immediately appreciated the difference between those two states. As an anchoring star of the show, his ideas were taken seriously by the creative team and were incorporated into the series. Still, he *did* have to be reminded to take it down a few notches—while *Gilmore Girls* demanded a lightning-fast, screwball pace to its dialogue, *The O.C.* would require pregnant pauses and more modulation.

"I talk pretty fast normally," he told the *New York Post,* "but it's nice—the luxury of being able to take a breath!"

Just before the series was shot, Adam was able to dash off a feature film called *Grind*. Adam had had inconsequential roles in several forgettable flicks like *Never Land* and *Roadside Assistance*. He'd also tasted the fun of being in a huge hit, as he was

Adam attends his *Grind* premiere with real-life GF Emily Montague!
(Barry King/WireImage.com)

with tiny roles in both *American Pie 2* and *The Ring*. He was more than ready to star in a major movie, and he felt the skate-boarding flick *Grind* was a good start in that direction.

Filmed in a single month, *Grind* was a film where its young cast banded together to offer advice on what was hip and what would make the movie better than the bare-bones script might allow. Adam had a blast making the movie, palling around with (and totally cracking up) costars Joey Kern, Mike Vogel, Jennifer Morrison, and Vince Vieluf. He was awed by the pro skaters brought in to invent moves for the film, and had very high hopes for its success.

> ∾ *"Basically, if* The Fresh Prince of Bel-Air *were a drama, this would be it."* ∾
>
> —*Adam Brody,* ELLEgirl

He told UnderGroundOnline.com that, "We got cast very quickly before filming, so skateboard boot camp happened on the set. Every day, we had a skateboarding park to ourselves and so we got free run of the place, which, as every skater knows, these places get crowded. So, to have these places, especially if you're not that good, and you're kind of embarrassed—you know what I mean?"

Unfortunately, *Grind* was an embarrassment in its own right. It received negative reviews from all corners (*Popstar!* magazine did optimistically call it a "riot!") and did dismal box office, making just over five million dollars.

The *Kansas City Star* earns the "meow!" award for saying that watching *Grind* "is like watching the dialogue portions of pornos."

Adam insisted to About.com that, "I think we took some liberties with the script and truly made it a little better. I think we switched some things around. There is a lot of crude humor in it, but there was more. We cut some out. And I like the flow of it. Here's the thing. When I originally read it, I thought, 'It's going to be funny, but I don't know how much you're going to care. It's a comedy. I don't really think you're going to care about these kids and their dream and making it at the end.' But when I saw it, I really think you do."

Showing he hasn't forgotten where he came from, Adam invited his old Spanish teacher (not that she's *old* herself), Ms. Morrill, to the splashy premiere of *Grind*, Adam's first red-carpet extravaganza. And he wasn't even *into* Spanish in high school!

It might not have done anything for his career, but it had been a noble experiment and, if you ask me, it's really a fun ride of a movie. Especially if you like gross-out guy humor. Oh, you don't? Well, apparently most of America agrees with you there. *Sigh*.

As *The O.C.* has taken off, those backhanded "geek" references I mentioned earlier have piled up, too. Adam, when quizzed what was meant by the whole geek issue, retorted that, it's "about me being incredibly *F*-ing handsome, and having to cast me because I'm also incredibly talented!" Yes, he was joking around. He's confident enough to know he's no total loser. Seth Cohen isn't either, but Adam feels he's "a little steadier on my feet with girls." In fact, he has a datemate in the form of the absolutely gorgeous (and incredibly lucky!) actress Emily Montague. [Insert sounds of angry pack of tween and teen girls chasing Emily out of town. JK, JK!]

When *The O.C.* was about to debut, Adam attended the premiere party at the Viceroy Hotel in Santa Monica. He felt like all his dreams were coming true. Josh Schwartz described him as a young Tom Hanks and the reviews almost universally singled him out as being *The O.C.*'s heart and its funnybone.

"Brody, who played Lane's boyfriend last season on *Gilmore Girls,* is particularly effective at bringing some lighter, more comedic moments into *The O.C.*," wrote the influential *Knoxville News Sentinel*.

"This may be one of the best months of my entire life right now," he told the *San Diego Union-Tribune* in reference to August 2003, "because of the show and the movie [*Grind*] coming out."

Now, Adam is enjoying the fruits of his hard work on *The O.C.*—he enjoys playing (just for fun) drums in what he calls a "wannabe indie rock/really bad Weezer" type garage band. Mischa and Rachel once attended a gig and goofily knocked over an amp while trying to play it cool. Bruised ego alert!

Adam is also known around Hollywood as a reliable moviegoing buddy, but he won't read a book unless its had seriously good things written about it.

He adores his fans, and was a popular part of a special viewing party held at Sharkeez in Hermosa Beach in early September 2003, where he met-and-greeted countless *O.C.* boosters.

But as he told the *New York Post,* "It's really weird to have it go from zero to sixty as fast as it did and to all of a sudden step out and have people say: 'Hey! The O.C.—love it, man!'" Also, Adam has had to get used to crazy fans crashing the set of *The O.C.* and doing wild things to get his attention.

Adam knows all of that comes with the territory, but he has also joined with Ben McKenzie and doesn't grant interviews and photo sessions with teen magazines. The guys posed for what will probably be their last teen outlet when they and Mischa appeared on the cover of *ym* magazine. The beachy

They look so cute together, even in real life! *(Jeff Vespa/WireImage.com)*

shot was *muy* unflattering, if you ask moi, and it probably didn't help that they quoted Mischa as calling Adam "quite the ladies' man." Hello! Girlfriend alert! But Adam was said to be a doll at that issue's launch party—he even left with the magazine's entertainment department to hang out afterward!

It's okay if Adam doesn't do teen mags. I'd buy *Cat Fancy* if it had him on the cover.

"There's about six things I could be happy doing," Adam told the *Tribune*. "I'm getting really interested in politics. I could be in the FBI or be a detective. I think that's really cool, too. I'd love to work for a newspaper and do editorials and stuff." But he's also made it clear he hopes to be an actor—and a lead on *The O.C.*—for a long time to come. As long as that does *not* entail him pretending to be a high school senior at age thirty.

He told *Entertainment Weekly* that five years from now, he'd "love to be doing movies I care about. I don't mean that it has to be *In the Bedroom*—just a great script I think is funny or touching." He hopes to follow Topher Grace's lead and stick with a popular TV show while venturing off when possible to make important and/or good movies (Topher has been on *That '70s Show* forever but still found time to make a lasting impression in *Traffic*.)

All I know is that Adam Brody makes me wanna get up in the morning. Well, not really. But he sure makes my Wednesday nights more fun!

s t a r   b i o

CHRIS

CARMACK!

Essential Deets

Birth name: James Christopher
   Carmack
Born: December 20, 1980, in
   Washington, D.C., and lived in
   Rockville, Maryland
HQ: Santa Monica, California
Height: 6'1"
Weight: 175 lbs.
Hair: Blond
Eyes: Blue
Marital status: Single

Workography

TV
Recurring Roles
The O.C. (2003–?) Luke Ward

Guest Roles
Strangers with Candy (2000) Laird
   in episode "Invisible Love"

Telefilms
When the Smoke Clears (2000)
   John

MOVIES
None . . . yet!

Chris at the Festival of Arts in Laguna Beach—a work
of art himself! *(Gregg DeGuire/WireImage.com)*

THEATER
ZADOK MAGRUDER HIGH SCHOOL,
ROCKVILLE, MARYLAND
Guys and Dolls (1990s)
The Crucible (1990s)
Hello, Dolly! (1999) Cornelius
Washington Metropolitan Area
   Shakespeare Competition
   (1999)

ELEPHANT THEATRE, HOLLYWOOD,
CALIFORNIA
The Day I Stood Still (January
   2002) Jerry and Jimi

THE EVIDENCE ROOM, LOS ANGELES, CALIFORNIA
The Strip (February–June 2002)

LAURELGROVE THEATRE, STUDIO CITY, CALIFORNIA
Lament of the Moths: The Lost Poems of Tennessee Williams (early 2002–September 2002), Reader/Guitar, Fear

WORKING SPACE THEATRE, LOS ANGELES, CALIFORNIA
Original Plays by Joe Bonito and Tim McNeil (July 2003) Earl in *Small Days*

MODELING
Abercrombie & Fitch (2000)
CosmoGIRL! (2002)
Elle France (2002)
ELLEgirl (2002)
Guess? (2000–2001)
KIA All-Models Event (2002)
Lord & Taylor (2002)
Macy's (2002)
Target (2002)
Who.A.U.Korea (2002)
ym (January 2001)

"I'm a little nervous now that the show has caught on," Chris Carmack confessed to *In Touch* magazine in September 2003. "I've never done anything where I was going to be *recognized*."

But the hunky actor was either being self-unaware or was displaying his small-town modesty. In fact, he'd already done some very high-profile modeling gigs and had appeared in some well-received plays that made him the "It" boy of Los Angeles.

But he was right in that nothing he'd done prior to *The O.C.* threatened to make him a walking star sighting!

Chris was born James Christopher Carmack to parents James and Susan in Washington, D.C. Chris and his older bro Scott and younger sis Kate grew up in Derwood and Rockville, Maryland. He has described his upbringing as old-fashioned, steeped in "Southern hospitality."

He would later tell an official Bolt.com chat that Rockville is "nothing like Newport Beach, California. I liked growing up there, and I respect my upbringing in Maryland now, a lot more than I did at the time. I appreciate the values that I got there, or at least in my neck of the woods."

All his life, Chris was an athlete. In fact, he was so active he earned the too-cute nickname Scrappy!

Scrappy Carmack, thanks in part to his participation in organized sports like wrestling, football, baseball, and basketball, was widely known throughout Montgomery County as a friendly guy, someone who was quick to introduce himself, to make new friends, and to be up for some wholesome fun.

One of Chris's fondest memories is of his time as a camp counselor. (Can you imagine? The crush factor in that camp must've been ten out of ten!) He did the honors at Seneca Creek Day Camp for a number of seasons. He was so attached to the camp that he once made a grand gesture in support of it. In July 1998, Chris and camp friends John McArdle and Adam Saltzman heard that Route 118 was being dedicated in nearby Germantown, a road that made life at the camp much easier. So Chris & Co. showed up shirtless and body-painted as a visual display of support for the new route.

"We'd never been to an opening ceremony for a road," then seventeen-year-old Chris told the local paper. "We appreciate the road because it helps us get around so we don't have to go out of our way." Nice way to say thanks, huh?

❧ *"Carmack . . . has the easy charm of a golden boy."* ❧

—Los Angeles Times

Always up for new challenges, Chris explored newfound artistic impulses in two ways: he got involved in music and he got heavily into acting.

Today, Chris is a blues and jazz musician.

"The blues can make you the happiest man on earth," he said reverently to *A&F Quarterly*.

He plays the sax and also loves to spend time writing music for his guitar. "Most of my free time I spend doing music," he told *J-14* magazine. "Sometimes I'll go out into the bluffs on Santa Monica and just strum guitar with the sun going down. That really chills me out."

In high school, Chris was in jazz from his freshman year on

and later joined a band called Exhale. This offbeat unit described themselves, with tongue firmly in cheek, as a "no good bunch of jazz ragamuffins from da east side of Rockville," made up of David Dunn (vocals/guitar), Josh Klein (vocals/backup/"toilet scrubber"), Chris (alto/tenor sax), Catherine Vendetti (alto sax), Mike Atkins (bass), Ian Fisher (trombone), and Jeff Miklaszewski (drums/"skin flute"). You can tell from this short description that they were quite the jokesters. In Chris's bio for the band, he is called "funny," a fan of Fishbone, and single. This despite his rep around the school as a major heartthrob. (He once dated a girl named Megan, and the girls of Magruder have since had positive things to say about him as a gentleman on various Chris message boards.)

As I mentioned, another new challenge Chris sought out in the ninth grade at Zadok Magruder High School was something a bit far afield for a jock—acting. But as he did with all endeavors, Chris didn't just test the waters, he plunged in headfirst, becoming what he would later describe as a "drama geek." He joined the Magruder Drama Club and began appearing in all of its plays and musicals. One of the musicals he starred in was *Hello, Dolly!*, and pictures from that theatrical event are still easily found on the Internet.

By his senior year, Chris was elected prez of the drama club and enjoyed great popularity.

> ❧ *"There are few people better to work with than Chris Carmack!"* ❧
>
> —*Michael D'Anna, Magruder High School*

His drama instructor, acting guru Michael D'Anna, told me exclusively, "Chris was involved in many, many, productions. He started by competing in the school talent show his freshman year with a middle school friend, Shannon Angelakis (who graduated Peabody School of Music)—Chris played sax and Shannon sang. He . . . always performed a lead role and performed exceedingly well. Chris was a terrific participant—never egotistical and always wonderful with his fellow actors. He also was a backstage crew hand for the shows while he performed out front."

The reaction of one of Chris's classmates on a Yahoo! group sums up how he was viewed by his peers as an actor: "When he's a famous actor someday, I'll be able to say I took English and French with him in tenth grade!"

One of the strongest indications that Chris had not just an interest in acting but also real talent was when he won a prestigious acting contest at his school in February 1999.

In what amounted to an intense audition, Chris was required to perform a sonnet and a monologue from Shakespeare's challenging oeuvre. Judges Debra Munk, Sally Walsh, and Charlotte Boucher declared Chris the winner from among everyone else in the drama club, sending him on as the school's rep in the Washington Metropolitan Shakespeare Competition. Chris's sponsor was Michael D'Anna. *Alas, poor Carmack!* Chris did not win the Shakespeare contest, but under D'Anna's tutelage, another Magruder student would win the whole thing in 2001.

Still, that experience had been invaluable to Chris. The program is one sponsored annually by ESU (the English-Speaking Union of the United States), which is a prestigious group founded by Sir Evelyn Wrench in the early part of the twentieth century. The goal of the organization is to "promote scholarship and the advancement of knowledge through the effective use of English in an expanding global community . . . in no narrow attitude of race pride, in no spirit of hostility to any people." Having advanced so far in such a legit acting program instilled in Chris the desire not just to be famous or successful, but to be *good* and to work with good material.

Chris also spent a semester abroad in Florence, Italy, where he would later say he had less culture shock than he did once he moved to Los Angeles to pursue acting!

Freshly back from overseas, Chris applied to and was accepted by New York University.

Before leaving for college, Chris appeared in his first filmed role, playing a mildly egotistical theater jock in a little-seen film for Maryland Community Television called *When the Smoke*

Clears. As described by its creator, Kevin Sockwell, the telefilm is "a story about friendship, about how it can be gained and how it is severely tested by the use of drugs."

The sixty-five-minute shoestring-budget movie is an eye-opening peek at a very young-looking Chris's acting potential at that stage of his life. Chris is beautiful to look at, comfortable in front of the camera, and is compelling in the cautionary tale's humorous and dramatic scenes.

As Kevin remembers, "Chris ended up starring in it and I wrote two scenes just for him because I knew he could do it." (You know I'm gonna hook you up with the 411 on it! Kev sells quality VHS copies of the movie for $18.95, shipping included in the USA, at: Theraplay Productions, c/o Kevin Sockwell, 13100H Millhaven Place, Germantown, MD 20874. Checks or money orders made out to "Theraplay Productions" only.)

When I asked Kevin about Chris, I received an enthusiastic reply that is very common to everyone's personal impressions of Chris.

Kevin does not pretend to be Chris's best buddy (people have been known to do that when you get famous). "My contact with him has been minimal. The funny part is that even with that limited amount of contact, I could go on for *days* about Chris Carmack," Kevin told me. "Chris is the kind of guy that you want to talk about—anyone that knows him would feel the same way.

"Working with Chris was a director's dream. He was a solid actor, he worked hard, he was *great* on the set and he was always unselfish and smiling through the six weeks of long weekend shoots. He was never asked to stay, but he *always* stayed after shooting to help the crew pack up. I have a blooper tape of the film that is mainly of his antics. He is very funny and a very talented young man.

"Chris was very popular in school, but *totally unaffected* by his popularity. He does not consider himself anything special. I am certain that when he got to the O.C. set, they turned his temporary character into a permanent one in part because of his acting skills *and* his perfect demeanor and temperament on the set. I would love to work with him again."

With a positive experience in front of the camera behind him, Chris headed to NYU to pursue his education.

Once at NYU, Chris studied acting at the Tisch School for the Arts and also attended the Stein School of Business. Most important, Chris became a Stella Adler student. The Adler organization was formed by one of theater's most influential artists, the trailblazing actress whose name it bears. This

> *Actors Chris Has Said*
> *He'd Love to Work With!*
>
> Jack Black
> Cate Blanchett
> Bill Murray

school of thinking instructs an actor in what some call Method acting (*becoming* your character) and also espouses reading between the lines of a piece and attempting to portray the unspoken emotions that went into its creation. Clearly, Chris was taking acting very seriously, as a craft to be honed and philosophized about and not just as an attention-getting device.

But Chris was also a young, fun-loving dude on the loose in New York! One insight into his sense of humor at this time is a long-abandoned student Web page he created at NYU. On it, he lists his hobbies as "sleep, theater, saxophone, and ladies." Not necessarily in that order, I bet! He also identifies his appearance in the local paper for that Route 118 dedication as "my crowning achievement!"

Other points of interest on "Chris's Page of Destruction!!!" include his fascination with *Space Ghost* ("Brak is the man!") and a highly imaginative personal bio that claims: "I was born in a small shack off the coast of Ingawalia, which is a small island in the South Pacific." Perhaps he once starred in *South Pacific,* but he was not born in the South Pacific! "There were no humans on the island at the time of my birth, so a local group of migratory whales took me under their wing. Their maternal instincts kept me alive They fed me 2,000 pounds of sardines every day . . ." It goes on from there with similarly eyebrow-raising flights of fancy. Chris wraps up by saying, "I have died and am making this page in memory of myself from Heaven . . . dude, we can get e-mail up here, but HOL is just as slow as AOL!"

If you ask me, Chris has a future as a *writer* if he ever gets sick of acting!

Chris is unlikely to get sick of acting, but he did find a new hobby—modeling. In March 2000, one of Chris's buddies spotted a handout announcing a casting call for Abercrombie & Fitch. Chris didn't see himself as a hottie who could actually believably go by the nickname Abercrombie, so he wasn't interested—peer pressure led him to cave in and try out. He was of course selected and photographed by the great Bruce Weber, appearing in the controversial *A&F Quarterly* catalog entitled "Back to School" in various states of undress. That led to posing for Pablo Alfaro in spring of 2000 for the Guess? "Wailea" campaign, a massive rollout (with Megan Ewing, Adriana Lima and Chris Oprysk) that put Chris's sultry face and body all over shopping bags and billboards and in print ads.

> ❧ *"As handsome as he is on the outside, who Chris is inside is even more beautiful. He is polite, courteous, funny, skilled, level-headed, and as nice a person you could meet. His character on the screen is totally opposite who Chris Carmack is as a person."* ❧
>
> —*Kevin Sockwell,* When the Smoke Clears *director/producer*

Despite the good money and the taste of fame that modeling afforded Chris, he never enjoyed it. He would later pinpoint the lack of creativity (who cares what a model thinks during a shoot?) as a major reason that he never pursued modeling aggressively. Instead, he used it as a job and as a stepping-stone.

In 2000, Chris made a fateful decision. In the same way Stella Adler had severed ties with the New York-based Group Theatre in the late thirties and taken off for Hollywood, Chris contacted the Los Angeles offices of his modeling agency and requested work on the West Coast. That was it—he left school and moved to Los Angeles, intent on furthering his acting career.

Right off the bat, he landed a rare comic role as Laird in the

Comedy Central cult series *Strangers with Candy,* playing the same kind of bully he'd eventually do so memorably on *The O.C.*

Still, L.A. was anything but love at first sight. Chris was depressed by the city's lack of "honesty" and all the games required to get ahead in the world of acting. Luckily, Chris had a solid upbringing and a devotion to the art of acting as opposed to working for the sake of working. His modeling nest egg gave him a measure of freedom to choose projects carefully. A national TV commercial he wound up doing in 2002 was a lucrative, painless way to support himself. Known as an up-and-coming model when he was really attempting to get ahead in acting, Chris's star quality earned him this prophetic quote from CelebrityMale-Models.com: "Chris Carmack will definitely be a star with his resilience and dedication to his work someday."

Homesick, Chris registered with Classmates.com under his very temporary name of "Chris Bowen" (changing your professional name . . . another of those annoying games sometimes played in Hollywood) and reached out to Magruder "Colonels" with the message, "You used to know me as Chris Carmack . . ." But the truth is that his last name was the only thing that had changed about down-to-earth Chris, and even *that* was only for a brief period of time.

You might be as surprised as I was that a guy as talented and as beautiful inside and out as Chris would have a hard time finding work in L.A.—but he sure did! That's a testament to the fact that there are so many starving artists in Los Angeles, and only so many roles to go around. Chris later described enduring literally two hundred auditions before landing work. Less surprisingly, Chris's first acting gigs were on the stage, his second home.

Landing a plum role in the drama *The Day I Stood Still* by Kevin Elyot was a big break for Chris in January 2002. The popular Page 93 production was staged at the Elephant Theatre on Santa Monica Boulevard in West Hollywood. The play was described as "a contemplation about obsessive, unrequited love" by the *Los Angeles Times* in their favorable review of the work. In it, Chris played a dual role—a young gay man named Jimi and his father Jerry. Chris had no problem playing a gay role thanks to his belief in inhabiting all of his roles fearlessly, and that comfort resonated with the audience and with reviewers, who took notice.

 Celeb Embarrassing Moment!

> *Chris once got a callback for a part and decided to play the role all nervous the second time. He didn't get the part—the casting people thought* Chris *was nervous, not his character!!!*

Backstage said, "The most interesting performance, though, is Chris Carmack's as both the young Jimi, torn by the failure of his teenage romance with another boy at school, and as Jerry at about the same age, electrically alive with . . . his burgeoning sexual awareness. They're delicately etched and beautifully varied portraits of a father and son—as different as night and day but connected by a similar drive to live life to the utmost."

Chris was also a featured player in a long-running farcical play presented at the Evidence Room in L.A. called *The Strip*. Sold as a "campy, late-night serial," the show ran for half of 2002, keeping him doing double duty when his next big opportunity knocked.

> ❧ *"When people find out you're an honest person and live in L.A., you're like Jesus or something."* ❧
>
> —Chris Carmack, A&F Quarterly

Chris had become a friend and play-going companion of the actor and *Entertainment Today* theater critic Travis Michael Holder during their run in *The Strip*. Travis and Chris next teamed up in what would become Chris's most acclaimed acting gig, a Tennessee Williams tribute entitled *Lament of the Moths: The Lost Poems of Tennessee Williams* that played at the Laurelgrove in L.A. over a number of months in 2002. Chris's performance was strong as a reader and he even incorporated his guitar skills. *Entertainment Today* raved, "While Chris Carmack's guitar playing is admirable and his delivery is excellent, he raises his personal bar way up when he talks about 'Fear,' with its symbolic metaphors and images."

Travis would also give Chris a well-earned good review for his "knockout" perf as Earl in the one-act play *Small Days* by fellow Stella Adler student Tim McNeil.

All this good buzz did not exist in a vacuum—it helped to get Chris noticed and to give him confidence when plowing through those scores of auditions. When he tried out for *The O.C.* and got it with no problem, it was a welcome first major role. Little did Chris realize that it was not going to be another infamous pilot that got shot and never picked up. Instead, *The O.C.* would com-

bine his love of drama (it even has a Shakespearean *Romeo and Juliet* vibe) and his urge to perform for a mass audience. It was more than a big break, it was a career-maker.

As soon as the cast was assembled, Chris realized the true extent of his good fortune. "I can't think of a better combination of people to work with," he told *In Touch*. His feature in that tabloid was his first major star profile, and it invited readers into Chris's Santa Monica bachelor pad.

In the photos, Chris's

Chris was nervous at the premiere party for *The O.C.*, but he had the time of his life! *(Mark Sullivan/WireImage.com)* rented apartment is seen as homey and cluttered—it needs a girl's touch, I say! The two-bedroom, airy apartment has a nice feel, like the green-tiled kitchen and a steady sea breeze. His living room is a pile of southwest pillows, a canvas chair, his guitar, books like *Real Jazz* and studies of Shakespeare and Clifford Odets and magazines like *Entertainment Weekly* and *Rolling Stone*.

One thing missing from Chris's crib is a television—he doesn't have time to act on TV *and* watch it.

He describes his diet as including burgers, cookies, eggs, and chicken and is quoted in the article as saying, "My bed is so comfortable. It's so easy to conk out in it." Sounds like a great Hollywood pickup line! Watch out, girls!

Chris is single for now, but act fast! And be informed. Chris told *J-14* magazine that he isn't into manipulative behavior and flirting. "I'm not all about batty eyes . . . I think a great date would just be hanging out, getting some good grub, listening to some really good music." So keep that in mind when you meet Chris and ask him on your first date!

Speaking of girls, Chris has said, "I like a girl that can be fine on her own. She doesn't need a knight in shining armor to rescue her."

Chris, it's not that we *need* them . . . we just like them! LOL!

As you can guess, Chris's life has changed a lot since his ascension to stardom on *The O.C.* His schedule is radically altered, he's recognized on the streets (and is sometimes pestered by rude fans . . . guys, c'mon! Play nice!), and he has many more options for other TV and film and stage projects.

Yet humble Chris maintains that his only major change is that he doesn't *have* to be on the hunt for other jobs to support himself while filming *The O.C.* We know more has changed for him, but it's a great insight into his character that this is all he'll give up as being new and different.

With an outlook that grounded, it seems safe to say that Chris Carmack is on his way to simultaneous superstardom and self-fulfillment.

Q&A with Chris!

A totally exclusive interview with Chris!

Reprinted with kind permission from *Popstar!* magazine. Originally appeared in *Popstar!* magazine, November 2003. To order a back issue, call toll-free 1-866-539-5624 or write popstar@leisureholdings.com for more info.

Q: You were a jock in school. How did you get into acting?

A: Acting just kinda took over—theater did. I did acting and also sets and anything you'd do in theater club. Organized league sports just kinda tapered out.

Q: What is Luke like?

A: Luke! He's a privileged, entitled young man from the Newport Beach community. He's got a little bit of a chip on his shoulder and a bit of an attitude. He's got the girl and the car and his whole world set up just right and this guy comes into the community and messes things up for him. I originally auditioned for the part of Ryan but got called back for Luke. I'm more that type, but not in personality. I had two dozen different ways to do six lines, I did it two ways and I got it. I was psyched to just audition for it—it was such a great script.

Q: You got this huge part soon after you hit Los Angeles, right?

A: Comparatively, yes . . . it was about a year and a half. But a year and a half will humble you. There were a few times when I was planning on skipping L.A. because it was so rough. You feel like you're throwing it into the void working hours and hours on every audition and nobody cares. Your manager tells you the hard work will pay off but the payoff is invisible . . . until you book a role!

Q: How did you like modeling?

A: In modeling, you look so posed and silly and stoic, so I never get recognized from that. But it was a better job than working in the computer lab.

Q: Are you prepared for what might happen if *The O.C.* becomes a huge hit and you turn into a household name?

A: If you know how to prepare for that, let me know? [Laughs] I love sitting on the side of the street just playing my guitar. I love my anonymity. So I'm freaking out a little about it.

Q: Do you like your TV girlfriend Mischa?

A: Have you seen a picture of her? It's not too difficult to play her boyfriend. I've often played characters where I have to find things to love about people, and with her, it's not too hard!

s t a r   b i o

RACHEL
BILSON!

Essential Deets

Birth name: Rachel Bilson
Born: August 25, 1981 in Los
   Angeles, California
HQ: Los Angeles, California
Height: 5'4"
Weight: 105 lbs.
Hair: Brown
Eyes: Brown
Marital status: Single

Workography

TV
Recurring Roles
The O.C. (2003–?) Summer
   Roberts

Guest Roles
Human Target (1992) Extra
It's True (1998) Extra
   [unaired pilot]
*8 Simple Rules for Dating My
   Teenage Daughter* (2003)
   Gum-Chewing Girl in episode
   "Career Choices"
Buffy the Vampire Slayer (2003)
   Colleen, Xander's Dream
   Potential #2 in episode
   "Dirty Girls"

A child of the business, Rachel is finally achieving massive success with *The O.C.! (Dimitrios Kambouris/WireImage.com)*

MOVIES
The Wrong Guys (1988) Extra

THEATER
NOTRE DAME HIGH SCHOOL,
The Crucible (1990s) Abigail
   Williams
Bye Bye Birdie
Once Upon a Mattress

MODELING
None . . . yet!

Rachel Bilson is being introduced to America as a shallow ditz with a snobby streak and enough attitude to wither an entire pack of those popular girls we all know from high school. The real Rachel couldn't be further from her character in almost every way . . . she does love to shop, though!

Rachel was born in L.A. on August 25, 1981. As the daughter of a producer, she was raised in the business that would eventually become her livelihood. A writer, director, and producer with a lengthy résumé, Danny Bilson was known for films and telefilms in the action/adventure and thriller genre. He often combined his talents on projects, retaining a lot of creative control on such titles as *Zone Troopers* (1986), *Kung Fu: The Next Generation* (1987), and *The Wrong Guys* (1988).

That last credit is especially important for *The O.C.* fans. See, while it was the second movie Danny Bilson directed and the fifth he wrote, it was also the first movie in which his daughter Rachel appeared—that's right, at seven years old, little Rachel Bilson made her debut as an extra in *The Wrong Guys*. (This makes Rachel the *O.C.* cast member with the earliest professional "debut"!)

The Wrong Guys was a loopy eighties comedy pitched in the following way: "What *Stripes* did to the army, what *Police Academy* did to law enforcement. . . . *these* guys do to scouting!" Centered around the twenty-fifth reunion of a pack of Cub Scouts, the movie also made use of the tagline, "When they were passing out the brains, these guys were off in the woods." Unfortunately, the film was a complete disaster at the box office, despite offering Rachel her first taste of screen time.

This wasn't the last time Rachel's father used her in one of his own projects, more for fun than to seriously advance her career as an actress—this was not an Aaron and Tori Spelling

---

Famous People Rachel Admires!

Orlando Bloom
Johnny Depp
Cameron Diaz
Katie Holmes
Diane Lane
Stella McCartney
Britney Spears

sitch, here! Rachel loved the experience, especially when she popped up on the massively hyped Rick Springfield TV series *Human Target* at the age of eleven in 1992. While Rick Springfield seemed a natural for segueing into a TV role, the show suffered low ratings and did not last past seven episodes.

In 1998, propelled by the relative success of his syndicated series *Viper,* Danny Bilson produced a pilot with Paramount called *It's True.* The show, which featured Rachel, would have centered around a made-up TV tabloid show like *Hard Copy* or *Access Hollywood* called *It's True.* The concept had reporters uncovering a governmental conspiracy to keep certain news from the public. The pilot episode was entitled "The Rats of Rumfordton" and was shot in Vancouver (where many TV series and movies are filmed) over three weeks in 1998. Though CBS had high hopes for the series, it had a huge budget thanks to impressive special effects and was not picked up. In fact, the pilot itself never even aired—it became a hot commodity on the bootleg market.

Rachel was not deterred by her letdowns in less-than-stellar projects. She was attending school at Notre Dame High School in L.A. and thriving in the school's many plays. She also set her sights on getting some roles on established TV series, something she would accomplish after graduation and before landing *The O.C.*

Rachel has described herself as a Valley girl. Her popularity gave her access to a wide variety of students—she even met up with some of the kinds of girls on whom she would later base her character Summer Roberts. (Don't worry, ladies, I won't blow your covers!)

In school, Rachel was the life of the party, a girl who had a strong sense of humor. She would later refer to the whimsical comedy *The Goonies* as one of her fave films and became hooked

> ### Rachel's Fave To-do List!
>
> 1. Shopping—"It sounds so cliché!"
> 2. Music—Especially Jeff Buckley
> 3. Eating—Where does she put it?
> 4. TV—Even her own show!
> 5. Parties—Like The Teen Choice Awards and Teen Vogue party!

Rachel on the 'Net!

Rachel told Bolt.com in reference to her growing number of fan Web sites that she "was told that they existed, so I checked them out. It's definitely flattering, but a little bizarre. It's weird to see so many pictures of yourself, but it's cool!" Some of Rachel's biggest online advocates refer to themselves as being engaged in "Operation Summer" to get her face in more magazines!

on TV reruns of *The Cosby Show* and first-run eps of *Friends* and *Sex and the City*. This fanciful streak belies her acting talent; while she enjoyed fluff as entertainment, she also won praise at school for her gutsy portrayal of Abigail in *The Crucible*.

After high school, Rachel—in spite of being the daughter of a prolific producer—definitely had some dues to pay. Rachel went on countless auditions coming up empty-handed every time. On the plus side, she was sleeping in till noon. On the minus side, she was beginning to question her decision to become a professional actress. She had always known from a very early age that she was destined to be dancing, singing, or acting—she just knew she was meant to be an entertainer. It's just that the practical side of the industry was getting her down. This is very common among actors pounding the pavement of L.A. or New York—with so much competition, it takes more than sheer talent to make an impression.

In fact, Rachel did not land any TV roles until 2003, when she finally broke through with meaty parts on episodes of both *Buffy the Vampire Slayer* and *8 Simple Rules for Dating My Teenage Daughter*.

Shortly after that, she was called in to try out for a new nighttime drama called *The O.C.* She was more than familiar with the terrain, and she easily summoned up the character we all love (to hate), Summer Roberts. She was a shoo-in. And Rachel couldn't have been more excited by the challenge—her first major role!

"I love that she's really driven," she confessed of Summer during a Bolt.com chat with fans. "When she sets out to get something she wants, she gets it!" Hmmm . . . sounds familiar, no?

On-set, Rachel is said to be closest with Adam Brody. She often attends events with him— they went to the Van Cleef & Arpels Frivole Collection preview party and the TV Guide 2003 Emmy party, and Rachel also supported Adam at the premiere of his summer skateboard flick *Grind*.

> **Summer of Discontent!**
>
> Rachel and Mischa once played a prank on Adam—they painted his trailer with fake blood and crazy slogans, scaring the heck out of him!

Rachel and Adam, of course, shoot many of their scenes together or about each other's characters.

"He's definitely a lot like his character," she's said. "I tend to call him Seth in real life, actually! And he does the same thing to me . . . calling me Summer instead of Rachel after we've shot a scene together. He's not as dorky as Seth in real life."

But don't get any ideas! Cute as they'd be as a couple, as you've already read, Adam is taken even if Rachel is single and looking.

At this point, Rachel is just settling into her role as Summer Roberts, but she's also adjusting to the idea of being recognized constantly in public. So far so good—she has gotten rave reviews from autograph hounds, who report she is extra-gracious when her newfound fans approach her in public.

Sounds like she's got a bright future ahead of her!

star bio

SAMAIRE

ARMSTRONG!

Essential Deets

Birth name: Samaire Armstrong
Born: April 26, 1981, in Japan
HQ: Sedona, Arizona, is her home
   but lives in Los Angeles, California
Height: 5' 7"
Weight: 115 lbs.
Hair: Blond with dark roots
Eyes: Brown
Marital status: Single

Workography

TV
<u>Recurring Roles</u>
Trash (2003) Gypsy [unaired pilot]
The O.C. (2003–?) Anna Stern

<u>Guest Roles</u>
Party of Five (2000) Meredith in
   episode "Taboo or Not Taboo"
Freaks and Geeks (2000) Laurie in
   episodes "Smooching and
   Mooching" and "Discos and
   Dragons"
That's Life (2000) Brittany in
   episode "When Good Ideas Go
   Bad"
ER (2001) Tasha, TBX Greased-Pig
   Chaser in episode "Sailing Away"
Judging Amy (2001) Angie Becker
   in episode "Look Closer"

Samaire cut her hair and suddenly found herself
receiving more and better scripts! *(Rena Durham)*

The X Files (2001) Natalie Gordon
   in episode "Lord of the Flies"

MOVIES
Not Another Teen Movie (2001)
   Kara Fratelli
DarkWolf (2003) Josie
Would I Lie to You? (2004) Sophie

THEATER
SEDONA RED ROCK HIGH SCHOOL
*The Effects of Gamma Rays on Man-
   in-the-Moon Marigolds* (1990s)

MODELING
None . . . yet!

Samaire Armstrong is someone who is thanking her lucky stars that a TV show *didn't* happen for her.

Come again?

Thanks to the fact that a pilot she did called *Trash* didn't light the world on fire, she was available to return again and again as the beguiling Anna Stern on *The O.C.,* a show you should know by now (if you're reading verrrry closely) is quite a hit!

All-American girl Samaire was actually born in Japan, where at the tender age of five she began dabbling in sword training. I've heard of taking back the night but the idea of a five-year-old with a blade is enough to send me on a solo cruise to Tahiti!

She later told myFW.com, "I started sword training with my dad and a group in Japan. We continued it through the years. We traveled a lot. I was always the smaller white girl and I was picked on so I was in a lot of fights."

By the time she was a teen (the age she plays as Anna on *The O.C.,* despite being twenty-three in real life), Samaire had moved with her family to Sedona, Arizona. She attended Sedona Red Rock High School. A very active Scorpion, she was a major volleyball enthusiast. But her major preoccupation was with acting.

Samaire and friend Jourdan Green wrote a lengthy and impassioned plea to the school's boosters in defense of the drama league, which went by the name A Company of Wayward Saints. In it, they reminded the powers that be (or the powers that *were*) that the drama program was vital and that it was going in an entirely new and more experimental direction with their selection of *The Effects of Gamma Rays on Man-in-the-Moon Marigolds* as subject matter. This treatise is noteworthy (and makes for good reading) because it displays Samaire's early passion for acting and also her inventive nature. The girls devised a $200-a-head fund-raiser designed to raise $50,000 to keep the program alive.

Clearly, this was not a girl who was acting as a hobby.

She graduated in 1998. Then Samaire (gifted with an elegant and instantly memorable and SAG-friendly name) headed to Los Angeles after an uneventful year attending the University of Arizona.

"In your freshman year there, you are not allowed to act in any of the productions, but they have all these rules to follow, like you have to help the older classmen get dressed and wash their clothes before and after plays—kind of like a fraternity or sorority," she ruefully told E! Online. "I was like, 'Why am I wasting my time here? Why don't I just go out and do it?' I came out to L.A. for the summer, and I never went back."

Smart move! The U of A can wash *this*!

At this point in her career, Samaire was a brunette with long hair and a very *Stuff* look (a mag she eventually was featured in). This helped her secure some early parts on TV shows like *Party of Five, Freaks and Geeks* (don't get me started), and *ER*.

Her first feature film was the rather unfortunate bomb *Not Another Teen Movie,* which starred the rather fortunate hunk Chris Evans. Samaire was relegated to the thankless chore of playing one half of a pair of conjoined twins.

"It was as bad as it seemed," she sniffed to myFW.com. "They had to attach us in the morning and the makeup took five hours and we couldn't take it off between takes. Some days we'd have it on for sixteen hours . . . We'd have to share a restroom together."

She did, however, enjoy a plush trailer and an on-call massage therapist, her first taste of the good life. In 2001, she attended a fun, happenin', and very glitzy re-creation of the 1941 premiere of *Citizen Kane*. It was one of her first major Hollywood appearances, but it was overshadowed by the events of September Eleven.

Samaire was pleased when she landed a big part in a werewolf horror flick called *DarkWolf*, an effort that would later enjoy kid-glove ridicule at the hands of *O.C.* costar Ben McKenzie on his infamous video loop of most embarrassing jobs held by Samaire, Mischa, and Rachel.

"We shot at this obscure, old studio in the middle of the night. Someone had died there a long time ago, and supposedly the grounds were haunted. We'd walk around to freak ourselves out. One time, we were walking through the area where they keep the abandoned sets, when the lights went off and the sliding door slammed closed. Someone was probably playing a joke on us, but we were sincerely scared."

The movie itself is pretty scary, too. Pretty scary, indeed.

But Samaire is a positive person and someone who doesn't let life happen to her. So she hacked off all her hair, dyed it blond, and developed her own clothing line called NARU, which caught on among many of her actress friends.

Her new look had a much trendier vibe than her old, va-va-voom look, and she was immediately cast in Chris Thompson's *Trash,* a WB pilot.

Starring vets like Lisa Blount and Richard Burgi, and fleshed out by *Hulk* hottie Mike Erwin and *Undressed*'s Pippi, *Trash* took a long time to enter The WB's radar. The Romeo-and-Juliet-in-a-trailer-park storyline seemed to be solid gold, but it did not make the cut.

Samaire has insisted it was "a great experience." It was also pretty funny, like the time when they had a bunch of actors dressed as cops swarming the real-life trailer park it was filming in and a resident emerged smoking an illegal substance and drinking a beer. He announced he'd just always wanted to do that in front of the fuzz, cracking everyone up in the process!

Something Samaire always wanted to do was be a working actress, and after a high-profile appearance in *Stuff* in January 2003, she got her wish: She read for the part of Anna Stern and joined *The O.C.*'s elite population.

Even though Anna threatens to take my Seth away from me, I just love her on the show. I think it's because Samaire Armstrong is so strikingly pretty and yet so obviously radiates girl power and wit. She seems to be a good match for a character I'm reluctant to cede to any other chick.

Let's face it—if ya gotta be in a love triangle with a guy and a girl, you might as well have a real challenge and let Samaire be that girl!

Ten

LOOK LIFTERS!

STYLE HEIST

Note: No companies or websites found in this section have any relationship with the author or publisher. Unlike fashion magazines, this book is totally independent. Take all of these suggestions as my own personal picks. And, of course, as far as I know, most of the style selections here haven't actually been worn or used by the *O.C.* crew (on- or off-screen) or endorsed by anybody connected with the show.

Along with giving us witty dialogue and wicked music, *The O.C.* is also responsible for rallying style mavens with the faultlessly fashionable outfits paraded by its stars. The brilliance of the style quotient on *The O.C.* is that, unlike nighttime soaps of yore, the clothes, accessories, hair, and makeup are neither ridiculously showy (*Dynasty*) nor so bland as to seem nonexistent (*Melrose Place*). Whereas a popular show like *Beverly Hills, 90210* definitely made its mark on the trends of the day, you always got the feeling the actors were wearing whatever brands were the show's latest sponsors. The effect was an icky feeling of watching the rich and famous cavort in the latest fashions from the Quickie Mart.

The O.C. takes place in an area whose residents have enough money to wear just about anything. Instead of always wearing designer labels, the characters often choose to dress down, affecting a style that is actually quite attainable by mere mortals like you and me.

If you wanna be the first person to help establish the Orange County look in your school . . . [long dramatic pause] . . . you're too late. But with the trend in full swing and showing no signs of slowing down, there's plenty of time to co-opt it, making it your own decidedly cool fashion statement.

With this chap, I'm trying to cover all the bases, fashionwise. I'm going to give you some basic pointers on the personal style of each of the major "teen" cast members, list some items of clothing they have actually worn, and leave you with a firm grasp on how you might go about lifting their too-cool-not-to steal looks without Xeroxing them too directly.

Ultimately, style is a totally personal thing; it's not something you can buy or learn from a book. So take some of my pointers and mix in your own inspirations and the end result is going to amaze you and your friends!

Let's get trendy!

Girls!

If you want to mimic the classic, contemporary O.C. look, here are some things to keep in mind!

NAME GAME: Crucial O.C. Labels!

> Juicy Couture
> Betsey Johnson
> Calvin Klein
> Prada
> Vera Wang

WHAT A SITE: URLs for Stylish Girls!

Some of my favey-fave sites for locating chic-but-affordable (or maybe not affordable, but very copy-able!) outfits, all of which I discovered during the course of researching the styles of *The O.C.*, are . . .

> www.blueplatefashion.com
> www.delias.com
> www.girlshop.com
> www.shopbop.com
> www.tee-zone.com

ABOUT FACE: Beauty Products You Can't Live Without!

1. Don't let sun and sand erode your complexion! Load up on **Kiehl's Ultra Facial moisturizer SPF 15** ($15.50 at www.kiehls.com)!
2. A **ten-inch loofa sponge** ($2.50 at www.soap crafters.com) is the ultimate Cali bathtub accessory!
3. **Clearly Natural Exfoliating Loofa Sponge Soap** ($2.99 at www.drugstore.com) gives that fresh, seaside feeling!
4. To enhance meaningful glances, use a **shu uemura Eyelash Curler** ($15 at www.drugstore.com)!

Rachel and Samaire are rivals in *The O.C.*, but embrace similarly chic styles! *(Albert L. Ortega/WireImage.com)*

5. **BeneFit Lip Gloss in Incognito** ($14 at www.benefit cosmetics.com) or **Lancôme Juicy Tubes in Beach Plum** ($15.50 at www.lancome-usa.com) gives a classy shine for sun-kissable lips, regardless of which O.C. actress you're emulating!

MANE ATTRACTION: In Search of Killer O.C. Hair!

1. Your hair is the easiest part of your body to nurture into perfection—and to use to make a tasteful beauty statement. This product is a great staple and affordable, too! Try **Pantene Pro-V 2 in 1 Sheer Volume Shampoo + Conditioner** ($3.50 at www. walgreens.com)!

2. **Kérastase Masquintense for Dry & Fine Hair** ($38 at www.joybeauty.com) fixes hair that's been tanning along with the rest of you!

3. For a light hold that moves with the ocean breeze, you can't beat **Redken Glass 1 Smoothing Complex** ($13.95 at www.redken.com)!

4. They say it's not good to brush your hair out every night, but a top-of-the-line **Mason Pearson Bristle & Nylon brush** ($79 at www.beauty.com) will keep the tangles out even after a day in the sun, surf, and Santa Ana winds!

5. A **Paula Dorf Brow Tint Eyebrow Gel in Blonde, Red, or Brunette** ($16 at www.beauty.com) makes sure you won't get caught with eyebrows that clash with your hair!

BODY CANDY: Clothes for Those in the Know!

1. BIKINIS WITH ATTITUDE—You *must* have a stylin' swimsuit, and the classic bikini is a staple of the Orange County crowd. Pick bold suits with tropical colors, floral patterns, or eye-distracting polka dots. **Billabong** (www.billabong.com) is a great place to

start, but **Vix Swimwear** (www.vixswimwear.com) is a great place to up the ante, considering its edgy, body-art suits and bikinis! For pizzazz, try a tied-on bikini with low-hanging ties. If you can't pull off a bikini (never actually *pull* it off!), try a one-piece with a geometric look. Avoid solid-color one-pieces or you might wind up with that dated *Baywatch* look. Ew!

2. THE I'M-STAYING-OUT-OF-IT EVENING DRESS—Think of a dress that's light, drapes over (and doesn't hug) your body, and helps your tan glow with its deep brown, rust, or eggplant color. Plunging necklines work, but flashy cleavage does not—the O.C. look is about the body but is not about being trashy.

3. SHOES OF DEATH—If your shoes are the most expensive item in your ensemble, you can't go wrong. Strappy and elaborate statement shoes are a staple. For the beach, flip-flops in any intense color of the rainbow work wonders and provide some financial relief from all those **Manolo Blahniks** or **Prada Mary Janes!**

4. SECOND-SKIN SKIRTS—Remember all those miniskirts from *The Brady Bunch*? They're back! Short skirts in warm colors complemented by tops in more risk-taking patterns help complete any O.C. chick's look.

5. YOUR DAILY TANK—You can never own enough simple, brightly-colored tanks with fitted sleeves and scoop necks. They go with almost any skirt, capris, or your fave pair of worn jeans.

The O.C.'s Ultimate Female Style Idol Is ... Mischa Barton!

HER STYLE ICONS Jennifer Aniston + "Princess Mononoke" + Cameron Diaz

THE MISCHA LOOK!

B E A U T Y

1 STRAIGHT-SHOOTING HAIR Make sure your hair is superstraight and silky! This requires gentle shampooing and deep conditioning, plus using products to tame your strands. A good bet for happy hair is **ISO Reflect Shine Shampoo** ($10.50 at www.monsterhair.com). To flatten your locks if they're naturally wavy or curly, simply blow-dry them straight with a round brush. Keep the dryer on *low* so as not to damage your hair. **Neutrogena Clean 60 Second Hair Repair** ($5.99 at www.walgreens.com) keeps your hair hydrated and minky, like Mischa's. Add **Redken Vinyl Glam Mega Shine spray** ($14 at www.redken.com) to achieve that glassy, reflective quality.

Mischa loves form-fitting outfits that avoid being too sexy! *(Dimitrios Kambouris/WireImage.com)*

2 24/7 AGLOW SKIN For skin Mischa would envy, never use regular soap, always use moisturizer and prioritize with products containing sunblock. Not everyone has flawless skin like Mischa! If you're having a bad-skin day, start first with some creamy **Lola Concealer** ($16.50 at www.beauty.com). Keep in mind that concealer under the eye is a great beauty trick! As a foundation—if you even use any, since Mischa's real-life look often happens without a base—indulge in **Neutrogena Healthy Skin Liquid Makeup in Golden Bisque** ($10.99 at www.drug store.com). Along with diligent care of your skin, you can get glowin' with **Laura Mercier Pressed Powder** ($28 at www. neimanmarcus.com). A healthy tan is an *O.C.* staple, but exposure to the sun's rays is always *bad*. And finally, shield your skin from radiation and instead mist yourself with **Phytomer BronzInstant Self-Tanning Spray** ($35.50 at www.sephora.com). If you're not tanning and for a sophisticated evening flush, try **Physicians Formula Retro Glow Illuminating Blush in Vintage Rosé** ($9.69 at www.duanereade.com) or **Neutrogena Soft Color blush in Divine Wine** ($8.99 at www.drugstore.com). An everyday blush Mischa has been known to use is **Neutrogena Shimmer Sheers in Mystified** ($8.99 at www.drugstore.com).

> ❧ *"The show centers on wealthy teens, so we're trying to wear some pretty cool stuff. I love fashion and I was psyched when I saw what we get to wear."* ❧
>
> —*Mischa Barton*, Women's Wear Daily

3 THE MANNEQUIN MAKE-OVER Mischa's lanky frame demands a healthy, balanced diet with plenty of fruits and vegetables. If you're trying to lose weight, fad diets are a big no-no. Instead, consider the more sensible and rounded **Weight**

Watchers program ($14.95 monthly at www.weightwatchers.com). Never put too much emphasis on weight simply for appearance—always approach it from a health perspective and you'll be in step with those California girls. Ultimately, be reasonable; not every girl can achieve Mischa's proportions. If you're not her body type, don't force it.

Regardless of your frame, anyone would benefit from pampering herself with lengthy **massages** (only indulge with professionals) to loosen up and stand with confidence and with that relaxed and relaxing West Coast slinkiness. When it comes to your skin, cover all of yours below the neck in **Jaqua Honey Almond Body Butter** ($15 at www.sephora.com). Mischa's all about moisturizing: "I can't live without sunscreen—I wear it every day," she told *Lucky* magazine. She also digs **Neutrogena Norwegian Formula Hand Cream** ($3.99 at www.drugstore.com).

Room for Improvement!

If you're a girl (and I think you are . . .), the latest trend for your room is to embrace your femininity. Try soft pinks and adorn the walls with girlie bulletin boards like Bed, Bath & Beyond's French Memo Vertical ($12.99) and Horizontal ($14.99) Boards! (at www.bedbathandbeyond.com).

---

④ SECRETIVE EYES In general, you're going to use neutral eye shadows with subdued shimmer. Don't be afraid to use it under your lower lid for a romantic look. Specifically, black lashes are too bold for Mischa's daytime look. For the softer look of a love goddess, opt for **Awake Stardom Optic Force Mascara in Venus Brown** ($28 at www.beauty.com). Evenings call for high drama, and just in case that drama leads to soap-operatic tears, you can't lose with **NARS Waterproof Mascara in Black Orchid** ($20 at www.sephora.com). A classic Barton shadow choice? **T. LeClerc Mono Eye Shadow in Violet Mystique** ($23 at www.eluxury.com).

(5) DYING-TO-BE-KISSED LIPS For lips that the Benjamin McKenzie in *your* life can't resist, you can't pass up the pale pink perfection that you get from **Lancôme Sheer Magnétic in Mischievous** ($19.50 at www.lancome-usa.com). More generally, Mischa's lips benefit from gobs of lip balm, neutral or pastel shades of gloss, and lipstick and liner in soft flesh tones. An ideal "no makeup" lip gloss is **Dior Addict Ultra-Gloss in Bite of Toffee** ($22 at www.sephora.com). According to *Lucky* magazine, a gloss that Mischa has actually used is **Neutrogena MoistureShine Gloss in Groove** ($6.29 at www.drugstore.com).

> ❧ *"I like dressing up, but I'd more likely be found in a Calvin Klein tank top. I also like shopping for designer stuff like Calvin Klein, Club Monaco, and also DKNY. Thrift-shopping can be great! I don't worry about dressing up in true Hollywood style."* ❧
>
> —*Mischa Barton*, Teen Celebrity

FASHION

(1) ATTENTION-GRABBING HALTER TOPS Whether we're talking about simple tops or even halter dresses, Mischa has the lovely shoulders and great form for this look. Check out the **ruby shimmer halter dress from Laundry by Shelli Segal** ($250 from shop.store.yahoo.com/edressme/roshhadr.html) if you're looking for a big-ticket staple. You can find more affordable halter tops at any major mall, but I'd suggest the **suspender halter top in black** ($54 at www.bebe.com) as an absolute can't-fail addition to your Barton-borrowed wardrobe! I adore the **matte jersey rouched halter dress with shark hem** ($44 at www.rampage.com)—another fine example of how you can look like a million for a few lousy bucks. The single hottest item is the **flounce red and black halter tunic** that Mischa modeled in

Lucky magazine ($42 at www.hotkiss.com)—the cheapest alternative and yet it's so cool!

2 LIGHTWEIGHT JACKETS WITH PANACHE Mischa wore her own **Dolce & Gabbana blazer** on the cover of *ELLEgirl* and also posed in a **cotton and nylon Alpha Industries jacket** that gave off a punkier feel ($95 at www.alphaindustries.com). You can copy easily with any light blazer in a neutral color, a vintage army jacket (nothing bulky or too distressed), or go off on your own tangent with a simple, fitted, pale-denim jean jacket!

3 DESIGNER CHIC Dude, Mischa Barton wore **Chanel** to her senior prom. She loves **Marc Jacobs, Diane von Furstenberg,** and **DKNY.** She's a big booster among Hollywood's younger set of hot designer **Zac Posen**, who she wore to the Styles 2003 Fashion Show at the Hammerstein Ballroom on April 22, 2003, in New York City. Face it—the girl adores labels. Do your homework on the overall look of lines like these, and you should be able to mimic the vibes with items picked up at your local mall!

4 DRESSES THAT FLOW OR SHOW Mischa wore a signature flowy, yellow dress to *ym*

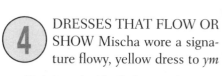
Mischa's penchant for slip dresses and light fabrics has created new trends!
(Lester Cohen/WireImage.com)

magazine's party celebrating her December 2003 cover appearance. Wearing a dress that clings only in the places where the fabric naturally touches your body creates length and communicates a SoCal "no worries" style. It's comfortable, fashionable, and can be extra-affordable! I found a **BCBG pink floral dress** ($259.99 at www.ifashionmall.com) that perfectly captures Mischa's daytime, softer look. But she does have a fashiony edge! For her *ELLEgirl* cover, she donned a **Sportmax Code cotton-stretch blend dress with lace** ($245), a dress that has more of an edge and shows more of her body in a trendy—but never too revealing!—way. And since Mischa's got such pretty legs, she showed them off in a **Bebe organza bubble skirt** (www.bebe.com).

> ❧ *"You never know who you're going to meet, and people want to see you look like you're loving it! I try to be a more glamorous version of myself."* ❧
>
> —Mischa Barton, Glamour

5 GOOD BUT SIMPLE JEWELRY Mischa wears jewelry, but nothing too chunky or glitzy. Instead, try to keep jewelry to a bare minimum and focus on a few spotlight pieces. You may want to check out the sleek necklaces and pretty pendants of **Jill Pearson's Wasabi Collection**, especially pieces with gold, ruby, jade, and pearl touches ($58–$168 at www.epinch.com). My fave would be the **cultured saltwater pearl on sterling silver snake chain** ($58). The ultimate Cali jewelry designs are from **Beth Orduña**, whose **18K-gold faceted ring** ($930 at www.zosaku.com) Mischa has actually worn. But if you're not exactly carrying any thousand-dollar bills around to drop on rings (if you are, the U.S. Securities and Exchange Commission might wanna see you!), you can also consider her **silver ring with citrine, garnet, and amethyst**

($245). Beth's chunky bracelets aren't very "Mischa," but her delicate necklaces are right on the money.

The O.C.'s Female Style Idol Runner-up #1... Rachel Bilson!

HER STYLE ICONS Catherine Zeta-Jones + Carmen Electra + Jill Hennessy

THE RACHEL LOOK!

BEAUTY

1 PORCELAIN SKIN Rachel doesn't have an English rose complexion, she has a perfect porcelain look that can be a challenge to achieve. I'd try **Cetaphil Gentle Skin Cleanser** ($6.49 at www.walgreens.com) on a regular basis, **Aveeno Positively Radiant Daily Moisturizer** *nightly* ($13.49 at www.walgreens.com), and **BeneFit You Rebel Moisturizer** ($24 at www.sephora.com) for daytime. **Neutrogena SkinClearing Concealer** ($7.49 at www.drugstore.com) will KO any imperfections, and if you gild the surface with **Neutrogena Shimmer Sheers All Over Color in Dazzled** ($8.99 at www.drugstore.com) for important occasions, you will out-Rachel even Rachel herself!

2 INTIMIDATING EYES Rachel has eyes that mean business! Traffic in that commodity by applying four or even five coats of a curling and lengthening mascara along the lines of **Maybelline Great Lash Curved Brush Mascara in Velvet Black** ($4.79 at www.drugstore.com). Moist eyelids complete this look. I would opt for **Biotherm Light Reflect Icy Reflect for Eyes, Lips, and Cheeks** ($13 at www.macys.com), which will keep your eyes heavy looking and the lids

saturated with shine and moisture. You can also use it on your lips or cheeks, as the name pretty much hints!

3 HIGH-BROW EYEBROWS You can't look like Rachel without precision-arched brows that communicate refinement and discriminating tastes. Pro waxing and shaping is a must, and try some **Personna El Perfilador Eyebrow Shaper Disposable Razors** ($2.99 at www.walgreens.com) for maintenance. They also help you in the bikini department!

FASHION

1 THE EVERY-DAY'S-A-PARTY PARTY DRESS Though Rachel Bilson is trim and fit, her fuller figure lends itself more readily to the average girl's body issues. Even if you're not boasting 5 percent body fat, you can indulge in one of Rachel's formfitting party dresses and look gorgeous—snug stuff on in-proportion-but-larger figures always helps accentuate the positive! Case in point, get va-va-voom with a **matte jersey empire dress with pink contrast details** ($46 at www.rampage.com). The black and pink combo is utterly Rachel! I also personally recommend the **BCBG black flower dress** ($236 at www.ifashionmall.com) or the **BCBG red dress** ($129.99 at www.ifashionmall.com), both great options for looking your most vibrant.

2 THINK TANKS Rachel is not about bah-humbug tanks, she opts for tanks in retina-burning hues like an **Allen B red halter top** ($128 at www.nordstrom.com). Want something to really make guys think twice about not giving you a second glance? Go for a patterned fitted tank or top that would fit in Rachel's closet and also on your happenin' bod! I love **Prana halter tops in Echo** ($37.95 at www.backcountrystore.com) for a dressy date or the **Patagonia seamless tank in Currant** ($35.95 at www.backcountrystore.com) for making the scene while shopping till you drop. You also gotta dig the **black shell with pink sash V-neck top** ($54 at www.bebe.com). And remember, Rachel has an award-winning back. Well, she hasn't *actually* won any awards for it, but it's definitely the *Shakespeare in Love* of backs. Go backless with your tops if you can for that extra Rachel Bilson *oomph*.

3 ACCESSORIES AFTER THE FACT Every girl wants one and you just know Rachel's got one: a **Louis Vuitton bag**. I like the **Marjorie** ($545 at www.eluxury.com), but then again, I don't have $545, so don't be shy to try a similar kind of bag that might have everything in common with the LV except for that logo. (Never try knock-offs, though. Ugh. Soooo Chino!) As for shoes, Rachel looks great in big, clunky, open-toed stompers like the **Paradise shoe in fucshia and yellow** ($99 at www.bebe.com).

4 TAKE-NO-PRISONERS SEPARATES Rachel looks great in dramatic formfitting skirts, jeans, and capris. I like the **French Connection sexy vintage wash cord skirt** ($40.80 at www.revolveclothing.com), **Joe's**

Here, Rachel pairs cute jeans with a glam sarong top, a look that could work anytime, anywhere! *(Steve Granitz/WireImage.com)*

Jeans miniskirt in the light H$_2$O wash ($102 at www.goclothing.com), and especially any **Elie Tahari skirts** (www.nordstrom.com). If you're springing for a more major purchase, I recommend an **Anne Klein petite contrast trim wool A-line dress** ($375 at www.saks.com). Hey, you can't take it with you! I also like **Lacoste capri pants in rose madras** ($95 at www.saks.com), preferably one size too snug, tee-hee.

SoCal Trend Alert!

As the icing on your Newport-look cake, try a cellphone ringer that plays "La Cucaracha!"

---

5 FEARLESS UNDERGEAR We seen how hot Rachel can look in **Victoria's Secret**—she filmed a scene for *The O.C.* wearing nothing more than a lacy bra (**Aubade blue lace demi-cup bra**, $89 at www.aubadeus.com)! No one is encouraging that kinda behavior in public, ladies, but wearing intricate intimates can sometimes give you a confidence that will show through your clothes even if your clothes aren't sheer. The trick is to look like you're probably wearing high-end things under every outfit you choose. Some of the frilliest and most elaborate examples are by **Mary Green** (www.marygreen.com) and they're not too pricey—just use common sense. If you're too young to buy a lacy bra without having to have it delivered to a friend's house to avoid Mom's detection, you shouldn't buy it in the first place. If you're not . . . then what are you waiting for?

The O.C.'s Female Style Idol Runner-up #2 ... Samaire Armstrong!

HER STYLE ICONS Rachael Leigh Cook + Drew Barrymore + Pink

THE SAMAIRE LOOK!

BEAUTY

1 PAINTED PEEPERS Of all the actresses on *The O.C.*, it's Samaire's that is the most cheerfully madeup. She uses a variety of glamorous and edgy products and creates dramatic eyes that eschew the natural look for the artistic look. Lashes deserve **BeneFit Bad Gal Lash Mascara** ($18 at www.sephora.com) and help your eyes pop with a **Sue Devitt Studio Eye Intensifier Pencil in Zaire** ($22 at www.sephora. com). Don't be afraid to experiment with shimmery or colorful shadows all around your eyes, like **Nars Duo Eye Shadow in Rated R** ($28 at www.sephora.com).

2 INSINUATING-SMILE LIPS Samaire has gorgeous lips that you can re-create with color, shine, and shaping at the corners if you don't share her Mona Lisa mouth! I like the smashing boldness of **Revlon Super Lustrous Lipstick Palette in Red Rocks** ($7.49 at www.walgreens.com) with **Anna Sui Lipstick in 403** ($19 at www.beauty.com) at the corners of your lips to create that deep-inset, all-knowing smile.

3 ULTRA-HIP HAIR Making short hair fun is Samaire's specialty—she has a kewt crop that makes use of brassy blond, dark roots, and a thick, choppy look that shows she is a trendsetter. "It's interesting how your look totally

Samaire in a cute tee that's oh-so-easy to find ... if you read this chapter!
(Jean-Paul Aussenard/WireImage.com)

dictates what kind of auditions you get or what kind of roles you can play," Samaire told E! Online. "Since the haircut, I'm getting all these lesbian scripts sent to me. I had really long hair when I first came out here, and I'd always get these really cutesy auditions. I was like, 'I'm not a sorority girl, guys!'" Brassy Samaire hair demands **Korres Calcium and Rice Proteins Coloured Hair Treatment** ($21 at www.lafcony.com) and lots of conditioning.

FASHION

1 SUPERCOOL CRUISE SHOES Whereas Mischa and Rachel might be found in high-end shoes, Samaire's kicks are more for kicks. Try matching that whimsy with a pair of shoes I bought myself while researching this tome: **Vans Chex Slip-On in Black, Aciano, and White** ($49.95 at www.zappos.com). I also like the looks of the **Steve Madden Opiumm** ($67.95 at www.zappos.com). Have fun with your feet!

2 DOUBLE-DARE-YA DRESSES AND TOPS To copy Samaire's dress sense exactly is to miss the point. But if you're looking for a rebellious and yet fashionable dress to impress, I'd say you could do worse than a funky, retro-looking **solid matte jersey dress with lace and satin trim** ($44 at www.rampage.com). A top that perfectly illustrates the Samaire ideal is a **grommet accent top** ($69 at www.bebe.com), with a wow-inducing one-sleeve construction and geometric motif. For those ultra-casual times when you still want to shine, I am in love with my **puff sleeve tee with flocked je t'aime screenprint** ($22.50 at www.welovefine.com) that Samaire has actually worn to an event!

3 ABSOLUTE ACCESSORIES The Samaire look can be easily accentuated with one-of-a-kind accessories, including a random array of one-dollar rock pins stuck to your denim jacket, a funky brooch from your mom or grandma's jewelry box, or a totally random pin found at a garage sale—the only rule is that there are no rules.

Guys!

Get your boyfriend into an Orange County way of thinking by helping him into an Orange County way of looking. It's much easier and more affordable for guys to achieve Newport looks—you might even get him into it without telling him what's up!

NAME GAME: Crucial O.C. Labels!

Billabong
Speedo
Calvin Klein
Level 27
MADE
Paul Frank

WHAT A SITE: DOT COMS FOR METROSEXUALS!

Sites for sore eyes, especially for guys looking to look good—you know who you are, you metrosexual you!

www.diesel.com
www.guyshop.com
www.tee-zone.com
www.urbn.com
www.vondutch.com

BODY CANDY:
CLOTHES FOR THOSE IN THE KNOW!

1 TRUNKS R 4 HUNKS You should not wear a bikini swimsuit if you're a guy, pretty much *ever*. It's okay if you're in Europe, where men of all shapes and sizes—even fat fathers and wizened grandpas—shamelessly wear Speedo brief suits to the beach or pool. But in Orange County, trunks—preferably the kind that kiss the knee—are much more de rigueur. The most revealing suit you'd want would be like the **European Swim Trunk** ($34.99 at www.undergear.com), but more like it is the **TYR Challenger Trunk with drawcord** ($22.95 at www.swimoutlet.com) or classic board shorts like **QuikSilver Zen Butter II Shorts in red** ($39.50 at www.nordstrom.com).

2 HOLD EVERYTHING UNDERWEAR With shorts always revealing peeks at the tops of guys' underwear, gone are the days when they could just buy generic briefs and not worry about ever being seen. Orange County flair is communicated by **Polo Ralph Lauren Tartan Boxer Shorts** ($13.50) or **Polo Ralph Lauren Logo Boxer Shorts** ($18.50, both at www.nordstrom.com). Guys can never go wrong with **Calvin Klein Boxer Briefs** ($25 at www.barenecessities.com).

3 THE SIGNATURE BELT Guys don't need a million different belts to accent every outfit—better to pick one or two that communicate his personality. The **Salvatore Ferragamo Reversible Calfskin Belt** ($165 at www.neimanmarcus.com) makes a stylish and sophisticated statement for any upscale look (it also says, "Dude, I am loaded!" even if he ain't). For a more relaxed approach, howzabout a cool **Itsus Seventy-Eight Belt in white** ($48 at www.goclothing.com)?

4 SERIOUS TOWELS In a beach-centric community, you should not be showing up to the shore with your old Mickey Mouse towel. I'd recommend a **Land's End 700 Gram Stripe Beach Towel** ($30 at www.landsend.com), which weirdly happens to quote from *The O.C.*'s logo design . . . at least to my eye! Or go ultra-hip with a **deluxe surfboard-shaped towel** ($28.95 at www.bettersurfthansorry.com)!

5 NOT YOUR DADDY'S VINTAGE TEE You can't be a hipster in California without a smokin' collection of vintage T-shirts. We're not talking about just old shirts—they've gotta be truly cool in color, content (the wackier the better), and fit. The best way to achieve Nirvana to a *T* is to troll Melrose Avenue in Los Angeles, where a variety of stores cater to nothing other than old-time tees. Old shirts come to L.A. to die (or get dyed), including college shirts, premiums, intramural athletic shirts, and coveted advertising tees.

The O.C.'s Ultimate Male Style Idol Is . . . Adam Brody!

HIS STYLE ICONS Jason Schwartzman + Jared Leto + John Cusack

THE ADAM LOOK!

1 SNARK ATTACK TEES Even more than Mischa Barton, Adam Brody has made *the* biggest fashion statement on *The O.C.* by being seen so consistently in a variety of impossible-to-miss-or-diss T-shirts. Often, they drip with irony (and appear to be freshly ironed), making Adam's chest a billboard for puckish wit. Try a grade-A retro **Atari T-shirt** ($12 at www.emerchandise.com) on for size, and don't overlook L.A.'s own **David & Goliath Tees,** especially the **Blue Devil** one ($20 at www.davidandgoliathtees.com). I also like the **Paul Frank Employee of the Month T-shirt** ($24 at www.urbn.com) and the **Paul Frank Space Camp tee** ($14.99 at www.urbn.com). The funnier, the more offbeat, the better—who can forget Adam's hamburger T-shirt?

2 WEALTHY-SLACKER PANTS Nothing too fancy, but the rumpled pants from a seersucker suit worn with a casual shirt says, "I'm loaded but not stressing over it." In jeans, you're safe in everything from the oldest, most legitimately worn pair of denims you already own to a pair of **Ted Baker Funseas jeans in indigo** (about $130 at www.tedbaker.com).

3 POLOS TO GO Adam looks great in what used to be considered the ultimate sign of total nerddom—the classic, schoolboy, striped polo shirt. The look, whether worn solo or with a complementary-hued tee underneath, now has a fashiony edge to it that is the fastest way for any dork to look trendy. To dupe it up right, get actual old-time shirts at **Vin Retro** (www.vinretro.com) for under $20. Try a **Hunt Club Narrow Stripe Interlock Polo Shirt** ($12.99 at www.jcpenney.com) or a **men's striped polo in green** ($14.99 at www.target.com). To more exactly copy Adam, don't pass up a **Penguin Earl Piped Polo in Navy** ($44.99 at www.penguinclothing.com), a **Penguin All Day Polo in Hillside Green** ($37.99 from www.penguinclothing.com), or a **Penguin Bunny Austin YD Polo in Faded Blue or Red Ribbon** ($41.99 at www.penguinclothing.com), all of which he has actually worn.

Stuff 4 Your Thumb That Doesn't Suck!

Some trendy video games to go along with the kind of lifestyle Adam personifies!

Tony Hawk's Underground (Activision) for GC, PS2, Xbox, GBA

Grand Theft Auto: Vice City (Rockstar) for PlayStation 2

Amplitude (Sony Computer Entertainment) for PlayStation 2

The O.C.'s Male Style Idol Runner-up #1... Chris Carmack!

HIS STYLE ICONS Ben Affleck + Casper Van Dien + Mark McGrath

The Chris Look!

1 MEGA-PREPPY HEAD-TO-TOE Chris looks too hot as a prep—it's a handsome style for guys with all-American lines. As a shirt, you can go as far out as a **Kenneth Cole Bed of Roses** shirt ($79 at www.kennethcole.com) or shirts by **Lacoste** or **Hunt Club**. When in doubt, go with any clothing by **Abercrombie & Fitch** and **Guess?**, both brands that were memorably touted by Chris in his modeling days.

Melinda Clarke shows she's a big fan of Chris Carmack's effortless style!
(Ray Mickshaw/WireImage.com)

② FOOT FLASHERS Of course, Chris's first choice on the beach (he lives in Santa Monica) is to go barefoot. Barring that, try a pair of **Birkenstock Nepal in Wild Rose Birko-flor** ($74.95 at www.birkenstockcentral.com).

③ PASTEL PIECES AND HAWAIIAN HEARTTHROBBIN' Chris is the kind of guy who looks good in everything, but every kind of guy looks just fine in a classic Hawaiian shirt—it forgives fat and catches the eye. Try the Orange County–local business Toes on the Nose for a **Pot of Gold Aloha Shirt** ($52 at www.toesonthenose.com) or a more conservative **O.L. Pareo Aloha Shirt** ($48 at www.toeson-thenose.com) for just the right colors and looks. Or try a pastel polo shirt or T-shirt under a **MADE Money Zip Hoodie** ($40 at www.madeclothing.com).

*The O.C.'*s Male Style Idol
Runner-up #2 . . . Benjamin McKenzie!

HIS STYLE ICONS James Dean + Russell Crowe + Matt Dillon

THE BEN LOOK!

① MUSCLE-TEE BASIC If you want your boyf to look hot, you can subtly help him dress more like Ben McKenzie. Losing the polo shirts and khakis will help make your guy less "cousin from Boston" and more of a bad boy. At least superficially bad. And hey, don't *actually* steal anything to re-create Ben's style—no boyfriend looks good in a navy blue penitentiary jumpsuit. The ultimate Ben statement is, ultimately, simple: any tight-fitting, dark T-shirt from any manufacturer. It's James

Dean lite and demands that you spend no big money—if it's expensive, it's wrong!

2 THE PERSONAL-STATEMENT JACKET Start out with a worn leather jacket from a thrift shop or a rugged denim jacket. But graduate to the **Volcom Youth Development Hooded Jacket** ($45.99 at store.swell.com).

3 STYLIN'-GUY ACCESSORIES Ben looks hot in those leather wrist cuffs, huh? To approximate that style statement, try the **Von Dutch Double Wide Embossed Leather Wrist Cuff** ($40 at www.vondutch.com). And hey, get a chain on that wallet, boy! Try the **Siver Cartel Wallet and Chain** ($24.95 at www.backcountrystore.com).

Eleven

O.C. ZODIAC KEY!

ZODIAC CHIC

Aquarius, "The Water Bearer" (January 20–February 18)

Stars Who Are: Paul Newman, Justin Timberlake, John Travolta

MISCHA BARTON
JANUARY 24, 1986

The Aquarius sign connotes intelligence and a cool carriage that often seems to reflect nobility—Mischa could be the poster child for Aquarians. Perhaps it's her British roots that Americans sense and see as reflecting an almost royal countenance, or it could just be that she has the kind of beauty that both men and women agree should be captured in art and entrusted to museums. The Aquarius is also bound to be someone with a scientific approach to life, an innate curiosity for how things work. While many go into technical positions, in Mischa's case this is manifested as a methodical and supremely well thought out approach to acting. They're also workaholics (check out this seventeen-year-old's professional acting résumé—which began at age nine—and you'll get my drift!) and quite high strung. Steam is let off by being hopeless romantics.

The Aquarius is likely to believe in love at first sight and to feel intensely for star-crossed love situations. When they settle down, it is often with a partner who is not only a love object, but also a social, financial, and resourceful equal. Mama didn't raise no fool Aquarians! As for signs, Adam is her most compatible costar, while Samaire, Rachel, and Ben are less of a match. Ben? Uh-oh . . . What does that mean for Marissa and Ryan???

Taurus, "The Bull" (April 20–May 20)

Stars Who Are: Cher, Shirley MacLaine, Barbra Streisand

SAMAIRE ARMSTRONG
APRIL 26, 1981

The Taurus is a party animal and the center of attention—and that's no bull! This is one of the most dynamic of the signs, but also very earthy. Pride and a strong sense of direction lead the Taurus toward financial security and also toward a wealth of experiences. As stubborn as a Taurus can sometimes be, he or she is also very willing to wait out any bad tidings or to work as long as necessary until a goal is accomplished. That's why a Taurus is a good match for the acting profession, where jobs can be separated by months and where it can take many years to become established. They're also born leaders: Samaire has exhibited this in her school years by spearheading drama league efforts. She also does it beautifully with her personal style by wearing distinctive, personalized clothing that marches to her own drummer and by opting out of the cheerleader look, cropping her locks for a more assertive and fashion-forward appearance. In relationships, the Taurus is less bull and more tiger . . . or *tigress*. People who have dated a Taurus often unfavorably compare future love objects to them! Based on signs, Samaire is least likely to mesh well with Mischa and Chris, but has a good chance of being tight with Rachel and Ben.

Virgo, "The Virgin" (August 23–September 22)

Stars Who Are: Richard Gere, Michael Jackson, Stephen King

RACHEL BILSON
AUGUST 25, 1981
AND
BENJAMIN MCKENZIE
SEPTEMBER 12, 1978

Both Ben and Rachel are Virgos, and that makes for a good working combo. Virgos are exceptionally practical by nature and are the types of people employers are seeking when they require "attention to detail." Another interesting thing about Virgos is that they tend toward having a highly

Adam and Rachel spend a frightening amount of time together,
like at his Knott's Berry Farm Halloween blast!
(*Albert L. Ortega/WireImage.com*)

personalized system of values and a rigorous set of ideals, whether it be in regards to morals and ethics or art and pleasure. In other words, they know what they like and they like what they know. They tend to be somewhat conservative in their personal demeanor, so while they're known to be highly creative and adventurous, it is usually within a safe boundary. They're not sky-divers, but Virgos will often find themselves investigating new experiences to see if they fit into what they're looking for in life. Virgos have such a refined outlook they are sometimes considered standoffish. But Virgos are not necessarily snobs. For Ben, this trait comes out in the form of his strong-and-silent vibe, and for Rachel, it's exhibited by her confidence and poise. If you start dating a Virgo, you're likely hanging out with someone who's faithful and loving—after all, if they've chosen you, to cheat on you would actually be an insult to his or her own taste! All signs point to Ben and Rachel being zodiacally close to Samaire, and not as close with Mischa or Adam. (But since Adam and Rachel *are* pals, they are bucking the universe on that so far!)

Aries, "The Ram" (March 21–April 19)

Stars Who Are: Victoria Beckham, Marlon Brando, Aretha Franklin

ADAM BRODY
APRIL 8, 1980

Rams are magnets when it comes to their personalities—who better than Adam Brody to typify an Aries? He has the classic traits of being ambitious and energetic, and everybody loves Adam, even if he can also be quite outspoken. (And would you believe sarcastic? Nah! Not Adam Brody . . .) The Aries is unafraid to chuck it all and start over or pursue a seemingly impossible goal, something Adam did when he traded his surfboard for a manager and set his sites on becoming a working actor. The downside of being an Aries is that

Adam is one of Hollywood's most popular new stars!
(Rena Durham)

they sometimes see everyone fawning over them and believe their own hype and get a little cocky. To many of us, that in itself can be endearing, but a little cocky goes a long way, so some sensitive souls get turned off to the showboat Aries—or get scared away. In love, the Aries is dominant and demands a partner who is at his or her level, but they're also very intense and are likely to have fun with silly relationship games like inventing cutesy names for each other or having private rituals and in-jokes that make the relationship fun and totally unique. Based on signs alone, Ben and Rachel would be Adam's least likely soulmates, while he'd be more likely to get along with Chris.

Sagittarius, "The Archer" (November 23–December 21)

Stars Who Are: Jamie Lee Curtis, Bette Midler, Steven Spielberg

CHRIS CARMACK
DECEMBER 20, 1980

Chris may be a former male model, but he's no space cadet. Anyone who knows him knows that, and it also fits with the model of the classic Sagittarius. Brainy in a philosophical (as opposed to scientific) way, Sagittarians are the ones who wow you with deep thinking and challenge your own intellect by bringing up issues you have avoided or never considered. They can come off to some as a bit high and mighty, but it's less about ego than it is about personal conviction—of which we know Chris has many. Sagittarians are seekers who are flexible on small issues and are hip to many different paths toward enlightenment. Music is a quasi-religious experience, and Sagittarians might delve into cultures far-flung from their own in an effort to get the big picture about life. In love, these folks can be kinda free and have affection for everyone. Frisky fellers! Tied down, they might be a little feisty for some partners to handle . . . but it'll be fun trying to tame them while it lasts! Based strictly on sun signs, Chris is most likely to get along with Adam and least likely to bond with Mischa or Samaire.

Twelve

WELCOME TO THE DARK SIDE

THE REAL ORANGE COUNTY EXPOSED!

> "It's not just a place, it's a state of mind."
> —*Orange County* (2002)

Now that you've been watching *The O.C.* and have fallen in love with the ritzy setting and all the pretty people (even the mean ones are nice-looking!), you may be interested in visiting the actual Orange County. If so, I want you to know what you're in for, so this chapter is full of the results of my spy missions to the real-life O.C. and its surrounding areas.

I hope you'll find it useful or, if the odds of you going there are slim to none, entertaining. Planning fantasy vacations that you'll never be able to take is a great hobby and was recently removed from the American Psychiatric Association's list of habits considered to indicate insanity.

There are 80,000 people who call Newport Beach home, but that is only a small part of the 3,000,000 who inhabit Orange County, which is made up of people from all walks of life. Of course, it's more fun watching a TV show about impossibly wealthy kids with serious relationship issues, so the focus goes in that direction even if the reality is more complex.

Welcome to Orange County . . . Newport Beach . . . *The O.C.*!

Orange Countdown:
A Timeline of the Whole Newport 'Hood

1870 S.S. Dunnells captains his ship *The Vaquero* into the bay and decides he's "discovered" a new area—he gives it the name New Port. The ship is almost immediately sold.

1878 Birth of Anaheim . . . Can Disney be far behind?

1888 McFadden Wharf constructed where Newport Pier stands nowadays. No yachts in sight.

1889 Orange County splits from Los Angeles. Birth of attitude.

1891 First area high school opens its doors in Santa Ana. Students are confused about who to look down on since there are no rival schools.

1892 Oil rush in North Orange County—fortunes are made overnight.

1897 First automobile makes its appearance in Orange County. It was not a Beamer.

1905 Balboa Pavilion erected.

1906 Pacific Electric Railway makes stop at Newport Beach, helping to expand the area.

1906 Newport Beach is incorporated—population under five hundred. Started small, just like *The O.C.,* but would eventually become huge, just like . . .

1907 Newport Island created by man-made canals. Even the island is fake.

1908 Tournament of Lights is inaugurated. Locals worry about harsh lighting conditions.

1909 Birth of Huntington Beach.

1917 Theda Bara's silent epic *Cleopatra* films key scene in Newport Harbor. All known copies of the film have disintegrated, save for a few feet donated to an archive.

1920 Newport Beach Public Library christened. Can you imagine the classic beach reads they must have in their collection?

1924 Birth of Corona del Mar.

1925 Speed of light measured through experiments on Newport Beach.

1926 Pacific Coast Highway constructed through town.

1930s Orange County becomes known as Second Hollywood with frequent appearances by John Wayne and Bogie.

1933 Massive quake in the area and "Laguna Woman" skull is discovered, establishing that the area has had inhabitants for at least 15,000 years.

1947 Beulah Overell trial in full swing, involving a woman accused and eventually acquitted of blowing her parents to kingdom come on their yacht. Lizzie Borden's methods quite antiquated at this point.

1953 Birth of Costa Mesa.

1955 Disneyland is inflicted upon the world in Anaheim.

1950s Ocean plots are selling for $10,000–$20,000. Now, that buys lunch.

1961 Launch of Newport Harbor Art Museum.

1965 First graduating class at University of California–Irvine. Totally awesome!

1966 First streetlights in the area.

1975 Massive Mariner's Mile fire that people still talk about.

1980 The notorious Crystal Cathedral is erected in Garden Grove. Holy crap!

1994 Orange County goes bankrupt but never stops dressing cool.

1999 Closing of historic El Toro Marine Base.

2003 *The O.C.* debuts. Locals yawn through diamond-ring-laden fingers.

O.C. A to Z

Angels: Anaheim's world-champeen baseball team.

AP: Advanced placement courses are de rigueur at CdM High. Being smart is as much a status symbol as being rich and being beautiful.

Barq's root beer: Local drink of choice, somehow trendier than a cola.

Bedroom community: This is what Newport Beach is, and it means *not* what you think, but that it's a community on the outskirts of a larger city.

> ### Balboa Cam!
>
> Want to check out some prime beach in Orange County? Surf to www.walknet.net/mylife.shtml. It's got several 24/7 cameras trained strategically all over the area!

Breakwater: Man-made rock formations that were designed to preserve the area's beaches. Not cool to horse around near them unless you are planning to wash up on shore.

Charity: Many functions are undertaken to help the less fortunate—which in the case of Newport Beach refers to all the rest of us.

Christmas Boat Parade: This annual tradition (held in guess which month?) lights up the entire Balboa area. Try keeping up with the Joneses' yacht!

Disneyland: The ultimate Orange County tourist destination, a place many Newport Beach residents would rather die than be observed entering.

> ❧ *"What you find is that Orange County could be like anywhere else and the teens have the same issues."* ❧
>
> —*Mischa Barton,* Women's Wear Daily

Fro-yo: In a weight-obsessed world where you're in a swimsuit half the time, frozen yogurt is the new Ding-Dongs. Or you could just eat paste.

Hotel rooms: There's a lot of them in Orange County—over 50,000 rooms.

Irrelevant Week: The last weekend in June, this irreverent celebration acknowledges the last dude picked in the NFL draft. No, really.

John Birch Society: Ultra-right–wing organization rooted in Orange County.

Legally Blonde: The oh-so-charming Reese Witherspoon filmed her oh-so-funny breakthrough movie in Orange County.

Master plan community: This is what Orange County was when it was founded, meaning that all the homes and streets were designed to conform, conform, conform.

Mighty Ducks: Anaheim's beloved hockey team.

❧ *"It's very interesting growing up in these communities that are sort of these planned communities with this veneer of idealism, but you come to realize that underneath the surface, there are dramatic lives."* ❧

—McG, CSMonitor.com

Newport Beach International Film Festival: A springtime fest that provides a great opportunity to become an amateur producer, to show off your digital masterpiece, or just to watch arty movies with a belly full of crab.

No worries: Hawaii invented it, but residents of Newport—especially the beach-bred younger set—have made it their mantra.

Novel: Start writing your novel on the beach. Talk about it. See how quickly you make friends.

Pfeiffer, Michelle: Miss Orange County 1978.

Punk: Rock movement from London that was embraced in Orange County by its privileged but bored children in the seventies.

QuikSilver: The nearly billion-dollar surf-focused brand that calls Orange County home.

Republican: The area is, historically, quite conservative in a "greed-is-good" kinda way, not a "repent-or-perish" kinda way.

Rodman, Dennis: Mr. Outrageous has a home in the area and co-owns Josh Slocum's.

Sand dabs: A seafood staple at any beachy restaurant in the area.

Stucco: The original homes (many still here) were stuck on stucco.

Surfing: If you can 'board, you'll never be bored in Newport Beach.

USC: The University of Southern California, an institution Josh Schwartz told the *Los Angeles Times* "Newport Beach kids are bred to attend."

Volleyball: The ultimate and sexiest beach pastime.

Wayne, John: Western movie icon who helped make Orange County fashionable during the Golden Age of Hollywood.

❧ *"Sure, we have parties, there's some drinking and smoking. But hard-core drugs? Not even close! A lot of people watch* The O.C., *but mainly to make fun of it."* ❧

—*CdM junior Tom Welch,* USA Today

Groovy Grub

Arches Restaurant
3334 West Coast Highway
Newport

A historic eats joint that features food made to order right at your table. A hot spot at Newport Beach with yummy cuisine.

———

Bayside Restaurant
900 Bayside Drive
Newport

Surrounded by art, you'll find yourself on a veranda eating with a full view of the crashing waves. A favorite among Newport Beach locals, Bayside Restaurant features a graceful island plantation decor, a view of Newport Bay, and an art collection that rotates every three months. The lounge opens to the veranda for those who prefer to dine al fresco. On Monday nights, patrons listen to diverse musical pieces performed by various pianists.

———

Crab Cooker
2200 Newport Boulevard
Newport Beach

This is *the* seafood place in Newport Beach for the young and fabulously wealthy. Don't be put off by that description—it's way low-key if you're full of sand and floppin' in your flips.

————

Dave & Buster's
71 Fortune Drive
Irvine

A primo spot for hearty food and also for fun and games—*literally!* This national chain loves providing kids with the latest cool games to play almost as much as it loves serving up satisfying food.

————

Josh Slocum's
2601 West Pacific Coast Highway
Newport Beach
www.internationalcuisine.com/JOSH/

Once a sleepy and safe place, this beachfront eatery has gotten all hot again under new management, including part ownership by Dennis Rodman. Do make reservations.

————

Mariner's Mile

Head to this yacht-clogged West Coast Highway village for the best lineup of seafood eateries in the nation. Too many to pick just one.

————

Sid's
445 Old Newport Boulevard
Newport Bay
Newport

The best spot for steaks if you're more in the mood for turf than surf.

————

The Stuffed Surfer
Newport Bay
Newport

Junk food burritos for surfers and surfers-at-heart who just want to refuel and hang ten.

❧ *"There is no culture to call your own there, because the oldest building in the community is younger than you are!"* ❧

—McG, TVGuide.com

Hip O.C. Locales!

Balboa Island
www.balboa-island.com

USA Today says this is the place "where there's a dock and yacht for most every home." In existence for less than a hundred years, this exclusive isle offers lots of opportunities—biking, shopping, yachting, or just a pleasant wander in the sun, sand, and surf.

Bristol Street in Costa Mesa

This sunny strip is where some of Orange County's hippest hangouts are found.

California Riviera

Hot resorts lining the Costa Mesa coast have been given this informal title. Ah, authentic Orange County culture!

Corona del Mar

A charming Newport Beach village with some amazing views from spots like Lookout Point and Inspiration Point, this is flip-flopville.

———

Huntington Beach

This is the best area to hit if you're a surfer, a surfer wannabe, or a surfer groupie! The perfect antidote to rage blackouts.

———

Laguna Beach

A cottage-dotted artist's colony with an idyllic shoreline.

———

Newport Coast

The homes on *The O.C.* would be situated here, in this mon-eyed, gated community on the ocean. Homes go for seven to eight figures. Gulp!

———

Newport Harbor
18712 University Drive
Irvine

A gorgeous small-boat harbor with scenic trails and some of the area's best beach houses.

———

Newport Beach

The snootier beach (c'mon, guys . . . it is!) when compared to the more chill Huntington Beach. Preppies are running around like sand crabs and the quaint little beach houses will set you back more than a mansion in most areas of the country.

———

SoBeCa

An area so hot it doesn't even exist yet. A rich developer hopes this moniker (inspired by New York City's TriBeCa) catches on.

It stands for "South on Bristol, Entertainment, Culture, and Arts."

> ∾ *"Nowhere else has it become more difficult to tell the difference between what is real and what is imaginary."* ∾
>
> —Ed Soja, professor of urban planning, UCLA,
> Orange County: American Hip Factory, *VH1*

Club Scene

Aysia 101
2901 West Pacific Coast Highway
Newport Beach

Part restaurant, part club, Aysia 101 is a great 'tude-driven spot to hear some R&B.

Chain Reaction
1652 West Lincoln Avenue
Anaheim

All-ages club features way-cool underground rock, punk, and emo from bands like Tsunami Bomb, the Ex Models, and the Early November.

Detroit Bar
843 West 19th Street
Costa Mesa
www.detroitbar.com

Ultra-chic lounge with killer DJs.

Hogue Barmichael's in Newport Beach
3950 Campus Drive
Newport Beach
www.hoguebarmichaels.com

A grown-up club with a rock edge.

———

The Hub Café
124 East Commonwealth Avenue
Fullerton

Serving up food and outdoor musical performances by local rock aspirants. Rollicking good times were had by all.

———

La Cave
1695 Irvine Avenue
Costa Mesa

The ambience-soaked basement lounge of this steak-and-lobster restaurant offers cool, cool jazz.

———

Sing Sing
71 Fortune Drive
Irvine

A silly-fun place where dueling pianists play classic rock tunes for you and your friends. Often degenerates into a sing-along. Dangerous stuff.

———

Rachel is a real-life O.C. girl—she has hit all of the area's hotspots!
(Rena Durham)

Hot Hangouts

Balboa Fun Zone
600 East Bay Avenue
Balboa
www.thebalboafunzone.com

Seventy years young, this ancient amusement park has a retro quality that makes it simultaneously cool and corny. Cute first-date location.

———

The Camp
2937 Bristol Street
Costa Mesa
www.thecampsite.net

A great retail space that offers an outdoor element if you're, like, a surfer dude, dude, and also cool shops inside. Super-devoted jocks from all economic backgrounds converge here, though only the rich ones drive away in their Beamers. Adventure 16 is *the* place for outdoor accoutrements.

> ❧ *"In Newport Beach, it's not as formal as Beverly Hills or L.A. Everyone walks around in flip-flops and eats their $60 entrées on paper plates."* ❧
>
> —*Josh Schwartz,* Los Angeles Times

Fashion Island
401 Newport Center Drive
Newport Beach
www.shopfashionisland.com

This is it, baby. This is *the* mall to haunt. With over two hundred stores, this massive mall has high-end stuff to browse and offers gorgeous Spanish architecture (red-tiled roofs) and views of the beach accentuated by elegant arches. Robinsons-May, Bloomie's, and Neiman-Marcus are to be found here.

———

Irvine Spectrum Center
I-5 at Alton Parkway or
I-405 at Irvine Center Drive
Irvine
www.shopirvinespectrumcenter.com

Riding the hundred foot carousel or shopping till you drop, this is always a place where it's easy to hang out, have fun and not put on airs.

———

The LAB Anti-Mall
2930 Bristol Street
Costa Mesa
www.thelab.com

Built in the shell of an abandoned warehouse, this chic, indoor-outdoor mall (sorry, *anti*-mall) has over a dozen shops and is as scenic as any locale that's ever had *anti* in its name. You'll find Urban Outfitters, Habit, Stateside, and other groovy stores, or you can relax in the central Living Room and just listen to music.

———

South Coast Plaza
3333 Bristol Street
Costa Mesa
www.southcoastplaza.com

This is the kind of upscale, traditional mall that the LAB is anti-. You'll find the likes of Vertigo, Eileen Fisher, and a Sony Style store. A good place to hunt for a prom dress or a gift for the girl who has everything. Don't miss the Orange County Museum of

136 / BRITTANY KENT

Art branch here (www.ocma.net); it's a cool institution specializing in local and modern pieces.

————

Triangle Square
1870 B-002 Harbor Blvd.
Costa Mesa
www.trianglesquare.com

The old reliable place to hang out, buy clothes, see and be seen.

O.C. Reads!

Orange County Register = **The standard**
OC Weekly = **The hip alternative**
Orange Coast magazine = **Covering the elite beat**

Hot Rides in the O.C.!

BMW convertible
Escalade
Jaguar
Mercedes SL500
Nissan
Range Rover
Volvo

Thirteen

WHO *TALKS* LIKE THAT?

TOP 20 ORANGE COUNTY LINGO LIST!

The O.C.'s Doug Liman told the *Sioux City Journal* that he "learned from firsthand experience with *Swingers* that you can come up with crazy words that are very particular to a specific place and, suddenly, people in Des Moines, Iowa, are using those expressions."

While that thought is so, so money, it's also true that the Orange County scene has always had its own unique vernacular, one that's just gotten a shot in the arm from the weekly ratings of *The O.C.* after already being revved up by the global domination of talkative exports like No Doubt.

Here is my take on some talk you need to be able to talk if you're ever walking the walk in the real-life Orange County. I don't pretend to have made up this slanguage, but if I did toss in some new ones of my own and kids start using them, I guess that makes me pretty gnarly, no?

Abercrombie: Tons of these run wild in Newport Beach. An Abercrombie is a gorgeous but terminally preppy boy (often blond) who looks like he just stepped out of the pages of *A&F Quarterly*—except with clothes. Can be a neutral tag or pejorative, as in, "You're such an Abercrombie in that polo shirt!"

Bitch: Derogatory term for a guy, meant to convey his perceived lack of worth as a man or as a human being. I think we all know the best line incorporating this one!

CdM: Corona del Mar High School is the real school on which *The O.C.*'s school is based, but it's uncool to say, "I attend Corona del Mar." Instead, try, "I'm CdM."

Cotillionaire/cotillionairess: Rich kid who might be found at a fancy ball or even coming out as a debutante. "Taking a limo to Chanel? What are you—a cotillionairess?"

Death breath: A nerd with whom it is loathsome to speak. "Keep moving, death breath."

Ew!: An exclamation that—importantly—must be spoken as if it has one half of a syllable. Means that something is distasteful, tacky and impossibly far beneath you. "Will I go with you to the prom? No!!! *Ew!*"

Gnarly: Like *shalom* or *aloha*, this word works both ways: it can mean that something is particularly cool or extremely bad. "Gnarly wave! Too bad it flipped your board and gave you that gnarly black eye." The word is so badly dated it's retro-hip.

Grill: Face. As in, "She got all up in that other girl's grill and that's how the catfight started in the first place."

O.C. Cast Quote— They Said It!

"He cannot shut up with the jokes, that man. It's hard to be in a dramatic scene with him, because he does these minute little things and you laugh. He's sort of wonderfully hyperactive. He's hilarious."

—Ben McKenzie on Adam Brody, E! Online

Heirhead: A young and aggressively hedonistic richie whose last name is the first thing they tell you about themselves. "The Hiltons are such heirheads."

Mommy hotness: The trend in an area of all the moms looking way young and datable to their sons' buddies. "The mommy hotness factor on this block is about a ten out of ten."

O.C.: Just plain old O.C., and *not* the O.C., is what locals use in place of *Orange County.*

O.C.er: Pronounced as a play on the word *seer,* this is a word that describes what—and who—you are. "Oh, yeah, I'm for sure an O.C.er—I never miss an ep!"

Pod people: A synonym of *Stepfords,* this is a description of boring peers or neighbors; people who live in cookie-cutter homes. Something that has been the trend in Orange County for fifty years. "I'm sick of all these pod people—they're just jealous because I have my own style."

Poolhousing it: Crashing with a friend, possibly for a long time or even indefinitely. "My mom is a drag. Mind if I poolhouse it with you a while?"

Rad: An expression of unparalleled approbation. Not only is the object of this adjective cool, it's cool in a way that almost redefines the word. "That Rooney concert was rad!"

Random: Not to be confused with random as in by chance, this term is both an adjective for something that is not just contemptible but totally out of step with one's world view, and a noun meaning an undesirable person, especially one of a lower caliber than one's self. "Check out those randoms in last year's Prada." Or "Why did I wear this? This T-shirt is totally random."

Stoked: Deeply excited from within, as in, "She's gotta be stoked that her boyfriend got her that ring."

Sup, foo?: A greeting that is phonetically derived from "What's up, fool?" and, more important, is an example of mocking your own ghetto *un*fabulousness so mercilessly that it actually gives you street cred.

That's awesome: An expression of disdain for something. Should follow an observation and be uttered as dryly as possible. As in, "Pop quiz. That's awesome."

X-Man: A comic-book nerd. "Are you an X-Man, or do you actually date?"

Fourteen

POP QUIZ

TEST YOUR KNOWLEDGE!

If you think you're a real know-it-all *O.C.* prodigy, why not put yourself to the test? This is not the kind of test you want to stop taking in the middle, even if it's an emergency—so get comfy and clear your mind for a major *O.C.* I.Q. exam.

(1) On which FOX TV show did Ashley "Holly" Hartman first appear?

(2) As seen in many Orange County backyards, what is the proper name for the kind of pool whose surface appears level with the horizon?

(3) Airing a thirty-second commercial during the first seven episodes of *The O.C.* would have cost you how much? (A) $10,500 (B) $115,000 (C) $375,000 (D) $1.2 million

(4) Which *O.C.* cast member was embroiled in a controversy in real life for posing topless while underage?

(5) Which cast member's first name is not their birth name? (A) Ben McKenzie (B) Mischa Barton (C) Chris Carmack (D) Samaire Armstrong

(6) What famous TV actress was once Tate Donovan's real-life girlfriend?

(7) Out of all the main actors on *The O.C.*, who is the only Canadian?

(8) Who was the first actor cast on the show?

(9) Who is the only real-life teenager among the show's stars?

(10) What TV show won the time slot the night *The O.C.* first aired?

(11) Which three cast members posed for the cover of *ym* magazine's December 2003 issue?

(12) Whose fave band is Death Cab for Cutie?

(13) Which O.C. actress has made a guest appearance on *Buffy the Vampire Slayer*?

(14) Which of *The O.C.*'s young cast was born in Texas?

(15) TRUE OR FALSE: *The O.C.* was banned from a local Newport Beach TV station for being "culturally inflammatory and derogatory to our viewers"?

(16) What acclaimed young actor was a member of "California"-singing band Phantom Planet?

(17) Adam Brody's movie *Grind* opened at what number on the Top 20 at the box office?

(18) On what night of the week was *The O.C.* originally scheduled to air beginning in the fall of 2003?

(19) *The O.C.* series creator Josh Schwartz hails from what state?

(20) What global tourist attraction is rooted in Orange County?

Answers

(1) Ashley Hartman decided to audition for *American Idol* on a lark. She had zero performing experience before her tryout. She made the Top 32 and was then called in to audition for *The O.C.* She, uh, got the part. But you *know* that.

(2) That would be your garden-variety infinity pool, and you're nothin' in Newport without one.

(3) The correct answer is (B) $115,000

(4) That was the usually demure Mischa Barton, who filmed the racy video "Addicted" with Enrique Iglesias—in which she removes her top—when she was seventeen.

(5) (C) Chris Carmack. Chris's real first name is James.

(6) Tate dated Jennifer Aniston and has a guest appearance on *Friends* to prove it!

(7) Kelly "Kirsten" Rowan was born in Canada.

(8) Peter Gallagher was the early bird.

(9) Mischa Barton is a bona fide teen.

(10) NBC's *Last Comic Standing* trumped the hyped-up *O.C.*, but our fave show gained viewers every week thereafter to become the hit it is today.

(11) Mischa Barton, Adam Brody, and Benjamin McKenzie gave *ym* their best fake smiles.

(12) Adam Brody's love for Death Cab for Cutie got the band's music featured on *The O.C.*'s soundtrack.

(13) Samaire Armstrong has taken a bite out of viewers on *Buffy*.

(14) Benjamin McKenzie is the Texan, ma'am.

(15) False, but amusing to consider.

(16) Jason Schwartzman provided Phantom Planet's celeb quotient until he left the group in 2003.

(17) *Grind* was grounded at number twelve the week it premiered.

(18) The show was set to air on Thursdays, and would have been head-to-head with *Will & Grace*.

(19) Okay, okay, Josh is from *Rhode Island* . . . but he did go to school in Cali, so he's got a right to write about the Orange County scene.

(20) That would be Disneyland. Ever heard of it? Cute place. Saw a big mouse there once, though.

Fifteen

INTO DUST

THE MUSIC OF O.C. AND *THE O.C.*!

Some hot TV shows have theme songs that mirror their hit status. When *Friends* became a cultural touchstone, "I'll Be There for You" by the Rembrandts became a massive hit in 1995. Other TV shows are less about one catchy theme song than about having a steady stream of hit-worthy music on their soundtracks, sometimes to the extent that CDs are released featuring music that has nothing else in common other than having appeared on *Dawson's Creek, Buffy the Vampire Slayer*, or *Ally McBeal*.

I happen to think *The O.C.* is in its own category, musically speaking. Why? Because not only is it presenting music to its viewers, it's *introducing* music to its viewers. The overwhelming majority of kids watching *The O.C.* had not heard of Modest Mouse or the Grand Skeem before tuning in. In this way, *The O.C.* is not just blindly branding itself with Top 40 tunes, it's taking a much stronger role as a musical tastemaker for a generation.

And the music is great! Thank God *The O.C.* isn't pushing Muzak, country ballads, or polka, because I'd still have to sit through it. Instead, I've discovered literally dozens of musical acts whose work now lines my shelves and about whom I think, "How did I *live* without this way back last summer?"

The O.C. has also teamed up with AOL to debut music videos on AOL's *The O.C.* Music Showcase, including "White Flag" by Dido and "Way Away" by Yellowcard.

If you've got rhythm or even just a hunger for cutting-edge music, join me on a ride through all my notes you hear on *The O.C.* week after week—and all the great music that's helped make Orange County a mecca for fresh beats.

That Theme Song . . .

I feel like you can often tell if a TV show is going to be good by its theme song. Whether it's *The Simpsons* or *Seinfeld* or *The Nanny,* if a show has a theme song that is totally, totally unique, it is a sign that the creators have taken extra effort. In the case of *The O.C.*, not only is "California" by Phantom Planet extremely striking when you stack it up against other theme songs, it's also musically edgy (unlike the examples I just gave). So it's not just a home run, it's a home run with bases loaded.

Phantom Planet is made up of Alex Greenwald (vocals/ guitar), Jacques Brautbar (guitar), Sam Farrar (bass), Darren Robinson (guitar), and Jeff Conrad (drums). Jeff replaced drummer Jason Schwartzman (the actor best known for starring in *Rushmore*) who was a founding member of the band but boogied in the summer of 2003. Their Epic Records rock CD *The Guest* united critics when it was first released in 2002—it's impossible to find any negative press about that album because it's classic, stripped-down rock with real attitude and humor. It didn't sell like 50 Cent or any-thing, but it featured the hot track "California," which was used in the 2002 movie comedy *Orange County.*

> *In Case You Were Wondering . . .*
>
> That groovy tune on the show's official Web site is "Mystik Circle" by Tom Kane and Colin Baldry!

Once *The O.C.* hit the big time, fans were so intrigued by the theme that it warranted a full rerelease of *The Guest* with all-new packaging designed to echo a high school yearbook, complete with signed dedications that are

2good + 2be = 4gotten. Alex said the November 4, 2003, rere-lease was "a way of saying thanks to those people who helped make *The Guest* what it was." It was followed recently by a second album from Phantom Planet, minus Jase.

Mischa Rox!

Series star Mischa Barton looks like a fragile flower, but her taste in music is a walk on the wild side! She has copped to loving mostly old-school rock, like sixties classics by the Rolling Stones and the Beatles.

Among more well-known current acts, she likes Radiohead, Good Charlotte, and Sum 41. And her edgier taste has led her

to acts like the reconstituted seventies punk legends Sex Pistols, the Clash, and also under-the-radar rockers Modest Mouse, Sugarcult, and Taking Back Sunday.

The camera loves Mischa . . .
and she loves the camera!
(Rena Durham)

THE SOUNDTRACK TO MISCHA'S LIFE,
AS TOLD TO *ELLEGIRL* MAGAZINE!

1. "Dancing with Myself," Billy Idol
2. Anything from *The Moon & Antarctica,* Modest Mouse
3. "Smells Like Teen Spirit," Nirvana
4. "Thinking About You," Radiohead
5. "Sweet Child O' Mine," Guns N' Roses
6. "Under My Thumb," the Rolling Stones
7. "Across the Universe," the Beatles
8. "Hey Jude," the Beatles
9. "Tainted Love '91," Softcell
10. "Seven Nation Army," the White Stripes
11. Anything by U2
12. Anything by the Clash
13. "Sheena Is a Punk Rocker," the Ramones
14. "Champagne Supernova," Oasis
15. "Wonderwall," Oasis

> ❧ *"Mischa seems normal, balanced and energized, though her musical tastes don't lean towards the typical 'N Sync or Britney Spears. 'No way, I'm not into mainstream pop. I can get pop from my little sister, Hania, and the classic rock—Rolling Stones—from my dad. I like everything. Even R&B.'"* ❧
>
> —Platinum

Adam Brody: Indie King!

Adam Brody, a surfer dude from San Diego, grew up immersed in the California rock scene that is being successfully distilled into episodes of *The O.C.* Because of Adam's expertise, writer Josh

Schwartz has actually taken his advice to include breaking act Death Cab for Cutie. In the same way Adam has turned Josh on to Death Cab, Josh—through his vision of Seth Cohen's musical tastes—has introduced Adam to Paul Weller's solo stuff and his work with the Jam and the Style Council, as well as Nirvana and the Ramones. Current bands Adam loves include Ben Folds Five and Bright Eyes. I also hear he has developed a jazz fetish that rivals Chris Carmack's, including a fondness for Chet Baker.

Ben McKenzie Music Matters!

Let's not forget that Ben is a fogey compared to the character he plays, so it's not like he's out there discovering random new bands with the kids. He told Bolt.com that vintage Stevie Ray Vaughn is more his speed, as well as De La Soul and A Tribe Called Quest. "I listen to the most random assortment of music possible. I'm from Texas, and Austin has a great blues scene . . . I'm also into the punk rock scene, some of the old-school punk rock like the Ramones and Bad Religion."

Ben's secure enough with his coolness factor to admit to liking what he dubs "folk/country kind of stuff." We're talking Lyle Lovett, not Dolly Parton and Toby Keith.

But in the you-can-teach-an-old-dog-new-tricks department, Ben says, "Adam Brody got me into some emo stuff, and I've been listening to some of the music from the show, which is pretty great."

Orange County Cool

Orange County has long been a headquarters for funky, rebellious, ironic rock music that is perhaps best described as a mongrelized (and some would say improved) version of classic London punk, New York new wave and Beach Boys flip-flop pop.

The Cuckoo's Nest in Costa Mesa was a very important venue that hosted punkers from 1978 to 1981 (it was demolished in 1998), and it was where influential bands like the Crowd, T.S.O.L., the Adolescents, Social Distortion, and Agent Orange could often be found. The Golden Bear in Huntington Beach was another seminal spot for Orange County's punk scene, but the punk music scene of Orange County was largely fanned by outta control yard parties since few actual establishments wanted the business of antiestablishment, anti-*everything* punk rockers, who could be violent and weren't, uh, good tippers!

Here are some O.C. gods and goddesses you need to take into account if you're exploring the sounds of the underground in the vicinity of Newport Beach!

#1 THE OFFSPRING

They formed in 1984 and a decade later became international punk rock icons with the release of the CD *Smash*. The Offspring are number one on the list because their catchy hooks have made them the most popular act out of Orange County, and frontman Dexter Holland is such a brainiac that he formed his own label. Nitro Records is a genius undertaking that now hosts vintage O.C. acts the Vandals and T.S.O.L. and fresher meat like Guttermouth and One Hit Wonder.

#2 NO DOUBT

The most famous ska band ever! Led by lead singer Gwen Stefani's Hollywood looks and the band's quirky stage performances, No Doubt went thermonuclear with their 1995 album *Tragic Kingdom,* a none-too-subtle pun against the confusement park that shares their hometown of Anaheim.

#3 SUGAR RAY

In the same way that No Doubt came out of nowhere with "Just a Girl" and "Don't Speak," so did Sugar Ray go from unknown semi-failures to household names with the release of "Fly," the lead single from their second CD. Lead singer and one-time teen idol Mark McGrath perfectly projects the group's "who cares?" 'tude, a great example of how trying too hard can sometimes be self-sabotaging while not giving a rat's booty can guarantee success. McG went to high school in Newport Beach with McGrath, who later told TVGuide.com, "I grew up in Orange County with McG, so to see his version of it on TV is *interesting*."

#4 T.S.O.L. (TRUE SOUNDS OF LIBERTY)

Launched in the late seventies as a take-no-prisoners punk rock outfit, T.S.O.L. was known for its shrieking anthems and white-painted faces. They became headliners and then TKO'd themselves when their music slowed down. Now, they're reunited and crunchier than ever! Their late 2003 disc *Divided We Stand* is a must-have. Jack Grisham of the band ran for governor of California, but he got punk'd by someone even more absurd.

#5 LIT

Fronted by bros A. Jay and Jeremy Popoff and rounded out by Kevin Baldes and Allen Shellenberger, this Anaheim-based rock act hit the big time in 1999 with "My Own Worst Enemy" from their platinum-selling *A Place in the Sun*.

#6 SOCIAL DISTORTION

Granddaddies of Orange County punk headed up by legendary outsider Mike Ness, Social D as they're called by fans has been rocking for over twenty years, combining anarchic punk with roots music and peppering its work with references to things most parents aren't way into.

#7 KORN

Huntington Beach-based band that made supposedly off-putting emo into gold by constantly touring and never letting down their fans. Korn, by remaining steadfastly anticommercial, wound up enslaving MTV and becoming one of the most lucratively merchandised acts of the 1990s.

#8 THE VANDALS

A punk band of the eighties that is known for its long, sloooow ascent to the top of its form, they're signed to Nitro and have gone from being golden oldies to contemporary masters of punk. Their official bio shamelessly states, "The Vandals are an unheard of example of a band slowly getting better and selling more and more records long after most of their peers have either broken up or just sucked so hard no one wants to even look them in the eye."

#9 THE ADOLESCENTS

"Amoeba," "Democracy," "Kids of the Black Hole." If you don't know these songs and you claim to like punk rock from the Orange County scene, you're majorly handicapped in that area. Legends in their own time, the Adolescents have kicked *A* on the scene longer than Seth Cohen has been *alive*.

#10 AGENT ORANGE

This band has an eighties vibe. Their music is more pop with its hooks and its surfer-chic undertones, though it's also got a bracing punk mentality to the lyrics.

Music and Musicians Who Have Appeared on *The O.C.*

EVERY EPISODE

"California," Phantom Planet
Original music by Christopher Tyng

"THE PILOT"

"Show Me," Cham Pain
"Sweet Honey," Slightly Stoopid
"All Around the World (Punk Debutante)," Cooler Kids
"Swing Swing," All-American Rejects
"Hands Up," by Black-Eyed Peas
"I'm a Player," the K.G.B.
"Let It Roll," Maximum Roach
"Into Dust," Mazzy Star
"Honey and the Moon," Joseph Arthur

"THE MODEL HOME"

"California," Rufus Wainwright
"I'm a Terrible Person," Rooney
"Caught by the River," the Doves
"In Your Eyes," Aaron D
"Do It with Madonna," The Androids
"Hallelujah," Jeff Buckley
"We're Going Out Tonight," Shady Lady

"THE GAMBLE"

"Wanna Be Happy," Brooke
"Sing Sing Sing (With a Swing)," James Horner
"Rain City," Turin Brakes

"THE DEBUT"

"Why Can't I," Liz Phair
"Lazy Days," Leona Naess
"Play Some D," Brassy
"To Sheila," the Smashing Pumpkins

"THE OUTSIDER"

"The Way We Get By," Spoon
"Sucka MCs," the Grand Skeem
"Eya Eya Oy," the Grand Skeem
"Let's Get Retarded," Black-Eyed Peas
"Brick by Brick," Grade 8
"Rock Like This," the Grand Skeem
"All Kinds of Time," Fountains of Wayne
"Rolling with Heat," the Roots

"THE GIRLFRIEND"

"You're So Damn Hot," OK Go
"Wait For Me," the Runaways
"Disco Church," the Faders
"Break," Palm Street
"More Bounce (in California)," Soul Kid #1
"Do You," User
"Hollow," Tricky

"THE ESCAPE"

"Good Day," Luce
"A Movie Script Ending," Death Cab for Cuties
"Out of Control," the Chemical Brothers
"Ritmo De Oro," Los Cubaztecas
"La Conga de Santiago," Los Cubaztecas
"Going Under (Kruder & Dorfmeister Remix)," Rockers Hi Fi
"Into Dust," Mazzy Star

"THE RESCUE"

"Keep It Together," Guster
"Let the Bad Times Roll," Paul Westerberg
"La Femme D'argent," Air

O.C. OBSESSIVES

FANS . . .
OR FREAKS?

No fan likes to be considered *too* much of a fan. You know, like how you hear people saying, "I'm a fan, but I'm not *obsessed* or anything . . ." as they nervously rock from foot to foot while standing in a room *covered* in memorabilia?

But something I've learned from chillin' with fellow O.C. watchers is that most of us are actually the opposite—we enjoy flaunting our devotion. I have come to the conclusion that O.C. fans put the "o" and "c" in "psychotic."

But for kicks, I gathered up some stories about casual, feverish and downright maniacal fans of *The O.C.* so you could decide for yourself on a case-by-case basis . . . FAN or FREAK? (My own diagnoses follow below.)

O.C. I.C.U.!

CASE #1: "THE VIDIOT"

She's taped every episode. Normal-sounding, right? But she also re-watched the first seven episodes every single day while the show was on hiatus. More than once. FAN or FREAK?

CASE #2: "COOPER'S SUPER DUPER"

This fan is well-grounded, highly productive, and a regular churchgoer. She never misses *The O.C.* now, but didn't start watching till the second ep because she hadn't heard about it. She loves all the characters but is mainly a Melinda "Mindy" Clarke fanatic. She's so into her she cries along with her during sad scenes and hoots appreciatively when Julie lands a zinger. FAN or FREAK?

CASE #3: "RAD DAD"

He's a forty-five-year-old married father of three who watches the show and knows all the characters' names. FAN or FREAK?

CASE #4: "MRS. BEN"

She's a huge Internet buff who's got screen names on every major service, from AO-HELL to Yahoo! to Earthlink. Under her profiles (but not in the actual screen names), she lists her last name as being "Schenkkan." FAN or FREAK?

CASE #5: "ALMA MATTERS"

She's a junior who just found out that Adam Brody went to her high school and graduated five years ago, in 1998. Upon learning this, she embarks on a fact-finding mission all around campus to speak with various faculty members who might remember him and in the process discovers one of *The O.C.*'s several producers has a daughter who had attended the same school very recently. Learning this, she further finds that the daughter now attends a different school, in Los Angeles. All of this information is stored mentally and also posted on *O.C.* message boards. FAN or FREAK?

CASE #6: "TANGLED WEBMISTRESS"

She's an unapologetic fan of *The O.C.* (with a special passion for Ben and Chris) who the week after the show debuted launched an elaborate, time-consuming, expensive fan site loaded with hundreds of pictures found in cyberspace and scanned from magazines. Because she felt the available bios of the cast members were skimpy, she paid a service a hundred dollars to get the home addresses of Ben and Chris and showed up with a tape recorder from RadioShack to request interviews. She didn't meet either, but she saw Ben once from a distance and almost passed out. FAN or FREAK?

CASE #7: "FORMERLY FANNISH"

She got hooked on *The O.C.* during its summer run, persuaded her family and about 75 percent of her friends to watch it, and then decided it was totally lame when the new season began in October. FAN or FREAK?

CASE #8: "DEATH CAB FOR HOTTIE"

This gorgeous dude is the most popular guy in his school and a major music buff. He despises anything mainstream and looks down on anything that is liked by too many people (ironic, since he is so popular himself). He would not be caught dead watching a show like *The O.C.*, except he found out the theme song was by Phantom Planet and then he realized the show spotlights the music of many underground acts. Now he watches the show religiously and, while it's ostensibly for the tunes, he stopped seeing his latest girlfriend because she once made an offhand comment that she didn't think Mischa Barton was *that* pretty. FAN or FREAK?

CASE #9: "SUMMER LOVER"

This guy has told everyone he knows that Rachel Bilson is his second cousin. His own last name sounds like "Bilson," but it's actually off by two letters. He sometimes carries a notebook with Rachel's picture drawn on it. FAN or FREAK?

CASE #10: "O.C. ORACLE"

She always watches *The O.C.*, having added it to her list of shows—her TiVo is doing double duty since she has over two dozen shows she watches without fail, many of them soap operas or soap operatic. Her extensive knowledge of such programs allows her to make spur-of-the-moment and yet faultlessly logical comparisons between *O.C.* characters and characters as diverse as the ones from *Passions,* old-school *Beverly Hills, 90210,* and even *Friends*. FAN or FREAK?

CASE #11: "SECONDHAND VIEWER"

He has watched the show under pressure from his female friends and thinks it's sometimes good, sometimes bad. He thinks Rachel Bilson is cute but seems like she'd be stuck-up in real life. He likes the music but rolls his eyes at the more dramatic scenes. He likes the jokes. He has missed about half of the eps and often asks in a loud voice, "Wait . . . who's *that*?" FAN or FREAK?

CASE #12: "THE KNOW-IT-ALL"

She's dutifully watched every episode and loves to surf sites for transcripts, which she has all but memorized. When hanging with her friends, the group often pipes up with fave quotes, but she will invariably issue a stern correction, even in cases where the incorrect quote has the same content as the correct quote, and is off by one or two synonyms. FAN or FREAK?

CASE #13: "PICTURE THIS"

She's a medium-popular girl at school who's known for having one fave show every year or two (*Smallville* was '02). She buys every entertainment magazine out there, even the really dumb embarrassing tabloids that only old ladies actually buy and hair magazines—if they have photos of the cast of *The O.C.* she will even buy a magazine that has one common publicity photo of which she already has fifty copies. She clips them out neatly and scrapbooks the entire show that way until she finds a different show to obsess over. (But she swears *The O.C.* is a show she'll never get sick of.) FAN or FREAK?

CASE #14: "ROAD TRIPPIN' "

She convinced her best friend to take turns driving from Michigan to New York in order to catch a glimpse of Mischa Barton, Adam Brody, and Benjamin McKenzie when they made personal appearances to hype the show in late October 2003. She got many digital pix of the trio near Rockefeller Plaza and brazenly talked her way into *ym*'s private party for the release of their December 2003 issue featuring the cast on the cover. At the party, she introduced herself to Adam and Mischa but missed Ben, and got photos and autographs from both of the stars. FAN or FREAK?

CASE #15: "MISCHA, TOO!"

She buys any magazine with original photos of Mischa Barton in order to copy down all the fashion credits. She then surfs to the sites or patronizes the stores listed in the styling credits and will spend up to two hundred dollars (but has her limits) to own any item that exactly matches something Mischa wore. By doing this, she has a week's worth of looks she can wear that mimic Mischa so closely it's totally Halloween.

CASE #16: "STERN WARNING"

This girl has had her name changed—legally—to Anna Stern. FAN or FREAK?

CASE #17: "FULL OF WOE"

She's an infrequent viewer of *The O.C.* who hangs out with girls who never miss an ep. By being around them, she knows as much about the show as if she'd seen it every week. She sometimes pretends to have seen all the episodes when she's with other friends, who don't realize her secret. She tells herself she does it to fit in, but she also wishes she *had* seen all the episodes. She just can't see them all because she has volleyball on Wednesdays. FAN or FREAK?

CASE #18: "I CAN STOP AT ANY TIME"

She has watched every episode of *The O.C.* and knows pretty much all there is to know about the main youth cast even if the grown-ups bore her to tears. She never talks about the show except when surrounded by accepting friends who have also seen the show consistently from the time it debuted. FAN or FREAK?

CASE #19: "BARTON FINK"

This girl has a bitter "I-like-Mischa-Barton-more-than-you-do" war going with an ex-friend. They both have unofficial fan clubs on the 'Net for Mischa, but the friend's dates back to *Once and Again* while her own site didn't make its appearance until the third episode of *The O.C.* had aired. The friend's site has many fabulous rare old pix of Mischa, some obtained by shady means from still other sites. Out of frustration, she sent e-mails to all the original sources for those images and got the friend kicked off her Web host. FAN or FREAK?

CASE #20: "THE FREAKISHLY FREAKISH FREAK"

She loves the show passionately and wrote an entire book on it in a matter of a few weeks, thus ensuring it would be the first one on the market. FAN or FREAK?

The Doctor Is In!

CASE #1: "THE VIDIOT"

This is normal behavior. If you like something, you tend to engage in it over and over again. This is a big FAN.

CASE #2: "COOPER'S SUPER DUPER"

This is a case of Cooper Stupor, where a fan is too involved with a baddie on the show. That's freakish enough. Worse, she didn't hear about the show until after it started with the hype machine it had going? FREAK.

CASE #3: "RAD DAD"

IMHO, any married dude who's watching along with all the kiddies is the father of all FREAKs. But he might also just be such a cool dad he's a FAN. I'm torn on this one, but would you want to watch any show with your dad staring over your shoulder?

CASE #4: "MRS. BEN"

It's very, very common for a FAN to pretend to be married to a beloved idol. As long as she doesn't register at Pottery Barn, she's normal.

CASE #5: "ALMA MATTERS"

This is obviously a FAN. Who wouldn't be ga-ga after finding out a star has orbited so close by?

CASE #6: "TANGLED WEBMISTRESS"

This is a FREAK in need of a leash! There is a difference between being an admirer and being a stalker, and it's not even a fine line. If you find yourself at a star's home, you're a stalker.

CASE #7: "FORMERLY FANNISH"

Anyone who believes the show jumped the shark as early as October 2003 is a FREAK.

CASE #8: "DEATH CAB FOR HOTTIE"

This guy's emo ego might be off the radar, but sticking up for your fave star and appreciating a TV show's soundtrack are both staples of being a loyal FAN. The real question is: Is he still single?

CASE #9: "SUMMER LOVER"

It's fun to pretend a star loves you, it's identity theft to pretend you're related. Rent *Six Degrees of Separation*. (No, Kevin Bacon's not in it.) This guy's a FREAK.

CASE #10: "O.C. ORACLE"

Annoying, maybe. FREAKish, no. This is a classic FAN of the variety you want to know in order to settle trivia disputes. Just don't get too close to her—her devotion is so intense it might cause you to question your own and put you off *The O.C.* prematurely.

CASE #11: "SECONDHAND VIEWER"

The key here is buried in the story—he thinks Rachel would be stuck-up in real life? Anyone with a brain can tell she'd be the opposite. FREAK.

CASE #12: "THE KNOW-IT-ALL"

This is a FAN, but without the cred that the "O.C. Oracle" from above has.

CASE #13: "PICTURE THIS"

She is not just a FAN, she is an old-school fan. This is the kind of person whose face is in the dictionary under the word *fan*.

CASE #14: "ROAD TRIPPIN'"

Though there is a mild stalkerish vibe where pursuit is involved, note that she only went after the stars in public places (even a private launch party is actually a public appearance) and once she caught them she was happy with a photo and autograph. FAN.

CASE #15: "MISCHA, TOO!"

Madonna had nine-year-olds in bustiers, Britney had nine-year-olds in halters, Beyoncé has them in low-rise jeans—couture copy-catting is a time-honored FAN tradition. Copying to the extent that the outfits are identical, lifted from magazines . . . well, that is FREAKishly close to identity theft.

CASE #16: "STERN WARNING"

Um, FREAK.

CASE #17: "FULL OF WOE"

This girl just needs a break—let's dub her a FAN.

CASE #18: "I CAN STOP AT ANY TIME"

It's FREAKish not to be into the adults since everyone I know agrees they rock. But overall this is a casual FAN.

CASE #19: "BARTON FINK"

This is a case of FANdom that has taken a FREAKish turn. Everything about her screams FAN, but when she took the step of trying to get a fellow FAN in trouble, that crossed over into FREAKville.

CASE #20: "THE FREAKISHLY FREAKISH FREAK"

I think this girl, while clearly a genius, is a FREAK.

Seventeen

BEVERLY HILLS, 90213

CONTACTING YOUR FAVES!

Wanna write fan mail to the cast of *The O.C.*? Try these contacts . . . and no, I'm *not* giving out home addresses!

Samaire Armstrong
c/o Mia Hansen PR
7700 Sunset Boulevard
Los Angeles, CA 90046 USA

Mischa Barton
c/o Pinnacle Public Relations
8265 Sunset Boulevard, Suite 201
Los Angeles, CA 90046 USA

Rachel Bilson
c/o *The O.C.*
FOX Television
P.O. Box 900
Beverly Hills, CA 90213 USA

Adam Brody
c/o Endeavor
9701 Wilshire Boulevard, 10th Floor
Beverly Hills, CA 90212 USA

Chris Carmack
c/o Jerry Shandrew PR
1050 South Stanley Avenue
Los Angeles, CA 90019 USA

Melinda Clarke
c/o *The O.C.*
FOX Television
P.O. Box 900
Beverly Hills, CA 90213 USA

Tate Donovan
c/o Gersch Agency
232 North Canon Drive
Beverly Hills, CA 90210 USA

Peter Gallagher
c/o Baker Winokur Ryder
9100 Wilshire Boulevard, 6th Floor West
Beverly Hills, CA 90212 USA

Doug Liman
c/o CAA
9830 Wilshire Boulevard
Beverly Hills, CA 90212 USA

McG
c/o Management 360
9111 Wilshire Boulevard
Beverly Hills, CA 90210 USA

Benjamin McKenzie
c/o Management 360
9111 Wilshire Boulevard
Beverly Hills, CA 90210 USA

Kelly Rowan
c/o PMK/HBH
8500 Wilshire Boulevard, Suite 700
Beverly Hills, CA 90211 USA

Josh Schwartz
c/o Zide/Perry Entertainment
9100 Wilshire Boulevard, Suite 615 East
Beverly Hills, CA 90212 USA

Eighteen

SURF'S UP

THE O.C.
ON THE WEB!

Don't be ashamed to surf the 'Net for *O.C.* info. You know what? Even its stars do it! "I really try to avoid it because it's a little strange . . . but I have, occasionally," Ben McKenzie confessed at a Bolt.com fan chat. "The good thing about fan sites is they're all so positive . . . if you ever need a pick-me-up. It's just really sweet and wonderful. It's really cool that people care that much about you to invest their time and energy into it, having never met you. It's amazing, and very flattering."

Top 3 Absolute Best Fan Sites

The O.C.: Official FOX Site: forums.prospero.com/foxoc/start
The O.C. Central: www.the-oc.org
The O.C. Online: www.fanbolt.com/theoc

20 Other Gnarly Sites

ADAM BRODY
www.adam-brody.com
www.fan-sites.org/adam-brody

BENJAMIN MCKENZIE
www.fan-sites.org/benjamin-mckenzie/biography.html
www.bmbrand.com
groups.yahoo.com/group/BMbrand

CHRIS CARMACK
groups.yahoo.com/group/ChrisCarmack
groups.yahoo.com/group/modelchriscarmack

MISCHA BARTON
www.geocities.com/Hollywood/Highrise/7547/MISCHA
HEAVEN1.html
www.mischabarton.net
members.aol.com/AAvante1/index2.html

PETER GALLAGHER
www.petergallagher.org

RACHEL BILSON
www.rachel-bilson.com

SAMAIRE ARMSTRONG
www.sweet-denial.com/samaire

THE O.C. LINKS
www.sirlinksalot.net/theoc.html
wborangecounty.tripod.com/foxorangecounty/index.html
www.devotedfansnetwork.com/theoc

ENTERTAINMENT SITES
www.etonline.com
www.imdb.com (*The Internet Movie Database*)
www.reel-style.com
www.tvtome.com

AUTHOR'S CLIFFHANGER!

"And that's all she wrote . . ." That phrase was never more appropriate than it is right here and now, as you wind up your journey through my catalog of, tribute to, and valentine for *The O.C.* and Orange County.

The reason the expression is particularly fitting here is that while this represents the end of what "she"—I, Brittany—wrote, rest assured that the true story of *The O.C.* has barely begun.

With only one summer and one fall season under its belt, *The O.C.* promises to be around for a very long time. Who will fall in and out of love with who? How many designers' names will be dropped? How many fistfights will break out at the drop of a—well, not a hat, because hats are so 1999.

Don't be surprised if you see an updated version of my book in the future as *The O.C.* builds on its already impressive history, and keep in mind as you watch our fave show, I'm watching it right along with you!

Thanks for reading!

Brittany
XOXO

—Brit

BIBLIOGRAPHY

All my sources and also resources for the reader to go hunt for
O.C. memorabilia and the like.

Magazines

A&F Quarterly
"The C.C." by Sam Riegel and "Orange Crush" by Guy
Cimbalo, Christmas Issue 2003
www.abercrombie.com

ELLEgirl
"Mad About Mischa" by Brandon Holley, November/December
2003

"Our New Crush: Adam Brody" by Maria Neuman,
September/October 2003
www.ellegirl.com

Entertainment Weekly
"2003 It List," August 2003
www.ew.com

Glamour
"How to Be the Next Big Thing" by Rachel Hardage, November 2002
www.glamour.com

In Touch
"At Home with Chris Carmack: Beach Chic Living,"
September 15, 2003
www.intouchweekly.com

Interview
"The Cat's Out of the Bag" by Scott Lyle Cohen, April 2001
www.interviewmagazine.com

J-14
"Boy Crazy!" December 2003
www.j14.com

Lucky
"Shopping with Mischa" by Charlotte Rudge, November 2003
www.luckymag.com

Movieline
"Cafe *au* L.A." by Lonny Pugh, May 2002
www.movieline.com

Paper
"Mischa Barton" by Britt Schoerhoff, October 2001
www.papermag.com

Platinum
"No Lolita" by Lois Ann Demko, 2000
www.platinummagazine.com

Popstar!
"Chris Carmack" by Matthew Rettenmund, November 2003
www.popstarmag.com

Seventeen
"Mischa Barton," July 2002
"Sugar & Spice," November 2003
www.seventeen.com

Shout!
"Can I See Your I.D.?" by Jordan Heller, February 2001
www.shoutmag.com

Spin
"Mischa Barton" by Stephen Rebello, November 2003
www.spin.com

Teen Celebrity [defunct]
"Who's She?" January 2000

Teen Vogue
"Up Next: Mischa Barton," Spring 2002
www.teenvogue.com

Time Out New York
"*Pups*" by Michael Freidson, February 10–17, 2000

Us Weekly
"Fall TV's 10 Sexiest" by Craig Tomashoff, September 29, 2003
www.usmagazine.com

Variety
"No Big Splash for FOX's *O.C.*" by Rick Kissell, August 7, 2003
www.variety.com

Venice
"Mischa Barton Picks a Winner in FOX TV's *The O.C.*" by
Steve Baltin, November 2003
www.venicemagazine.com

Women's Wear Daily
"Shore Thing" by Marcy Medina, July 21, 2003
www.wwd.com

ym
"O.C.: Obsessed Completely" by Ali Gazan, December 2003
www.ym.com

Zink
"Marvelous Mischa," February 2003
www.zinkmag.com

Newspapers

Austin American-Statesman
"Benjamin McKenzie's Big Break" by Diane Holloway, August 4, 2003
www.statesman.com

Boston Globe
"California Dreamin'" by Suzanne C. Ryan, August 5, 2003
www.boston.com

Calgary Sun
"*The* O.C. a Great Guilty Pleasure" by Kevin Williamson, August 5, 2003
www.calgary.com

Chicago Sun-Times
"*Pups*" by Roger Ebert, 1999

"Lost and Delirious" by Roger Ebert, January 24, 2001
www.suntimes.com

The Declaration
"Desperately Seeking Six" by Kristin Ricaurte, December 7,
2000
www.the-declaration.com

Gannett Newspapers
"Twelve Dreams", 1995

Gwinnet Daily Post
"Fox Puts Another California Place on Map," August 2003
www.gwinnettdailyonline.com

Kansas City Star
"Bad Comedy Blows the Wheels Off *Grind*" by Dan Lybarger,
August 1, 2003

"Soapy *O.C.* Is Hiding a Tender Center" by Aaron Barnhart,
August 5, 2003
www.kansascity.com

Knoxville News Sentinel
"Fox 'Fall' Premiere Leads Off August's TV Highlights" by Terry
Morrow, July 31, 2003

"Privileged, Ill-Behaved Kids Dominate *The O.C.*," August
2003
www.knoxnews.com

Los Angeles Times
"Deep in the Shallow End of L.A." by Howard Rosenberg,
August 1, 2003

"Love Unrequited and Lost in *The Day I Stood Still*," January
18, 2002

"O.C. Culture's Hip Replacement" by Kimi Yoshino with
contributions from Claire Luna, July 19, 2003

"Memorable Performances Power Offbeat *Lawn Dogs*" by Kevin
Thomas, May 2001
www.latimes.com

Miami Herald
"Engrossing O.C. Looks at Push-Pull of Life" by Glenn Garvin,
August 5, 2003
www.miamiherald.com

Milwaukee Journal Sentinel
"Fox Gets Good Jump on Fall with *The O.C.*," August 2, 2003
www.jsonline.com

New York Newsday
"One Flea Square" by Linda Winer, 1997
www.newyorknewsday.com

New York Post
"One Flea Spare" by Clive Barnes, 1997

"Best Debut Since George Clooney," August 5, 2003
by Linda Stasi

"Never Too Young" by Maxine Shen, August 25, 2003

"Adam Brody Talks About Being the Nerd on *The O.C.*" by
Maxine Shen, September 17, 2003
www.nypost.com

New York Times
"*Slavs!*" by David Richards, 1995
www.newyorktimes.com

San Diego Union-Tribune
"Local's Acting Success Reads Like a Screenplay" by Robert P.
Laurence, August 5, 2003
www.signonsandiego.com

San Francisco Chronicle
"*The* O.C. Tiptoes the Line Between Drama and Soap and Doesn't Lose Its Balance" by Tim Goodman, August 5, 2003
www.sfgate.com

Sioux City Journal
"Not All California Kids Live in 90210 Zone" by Bruce R. Miller, October 5, 2003
www.siouxcityjournal.com

USA Today
"McKenzie is Hoping to Stage a Hit with O.C." by Robert Bianco, August 4, 2003

"Greek Chic" by Susan Wloszczyna and Ann Oldenburg, October 23, 2003
www.usatoday.com

Village Voice
"Rich Kid, Poor Kid" by Joy Press, August 20–26, 2003
www.villagevoice.com

Washington Post
"*Lawn Dogs*: A Breed Apart" by Michael O'Sullivan, June 5, 1998
www.washingtonpost.com

Wichita Eagle
"FOX to Get the Fall Season Rolling Early with Its Juicy O.C.," August 2003
www.wichitaeagle.com

Web Sites

About.com
www.about.com

Bolt.com
www.bolt.com

The Cavalier Daily Online
"*Homecoming*: Where the Heart isn't" by Ben Nuckols,
November 2, 1999

"Pirandello's *Author* Loses Itself in Translation at Culbreth" by
Doug Strassler, November 21, 2000

"Modern Twist Breathes New Life in Classic Shakespeare" by
Lauren Pollet, February 19, 2001

"New Helms Play Uses Incarceration Issues to Reveal Search
for Identity" by Christina Buurma, April 26, 2001
www.cavalierdaily.com

Celebrity Male Models.com
www.celebritymalemodels.com

CNN Showbiz
"The Outsider of *The O.C.*," October 28, 2003
www.cnn.com

CSMonitor.com
"Lifestyles of the Rich and Under 18" by Gloria Goodale,
August 1, 2003

Curtain Up
"Life is a Dream" by David Lohrey, January 2002
www.curtainup.com

E! Online
"O.C. Does It" by Kristin Veitch, August 2003
www.eonline.com

"Who the Hell Is This? Samaire Armstrong" by Rhonda
Richford, October 10, 2003
www.eonline.com

Entertainment Today
Lament for the Moths: The Lost Poems of Tennessee Williams"
by Jose Ruiz, 2002
www.ent-today.com

Entertainment Weekly's EW.com
"It's Geek to Me" by Brian Hiatt, September 17, 2003
www.ew.com

ET Online
"Prepare to Enter *The O.C.*" August 1, 2003
www.etonline.com

The Green Room
"Mischa Barton," Issue 12, 2002
by Jason Burns
www.greenroommag.com

The Internet Movie Database (IMDb)
www.imdb.com

Jump the Shark
www.jumptheshark.com

msn Entertainment
entertainment.msn.com/

myFW
"The Ones to Watch: Part 5: Samaire Armstrong," 2002
www.myfw.com

The O.C. Central
www.the-oc.org/

The O.C. Links
www.sirlinksalot.net/theoc.html

Reel-Style
www.reel-style.com

ReviewPlays.Com
www.reviewplays.com

Script Sales.com
www.scriptsales.com

TVGuide.com
"The 411 on The O.C.'s MVP," August 2003
by Ben Katner
www.tvguide.com

TVGuide.com
"Welcome to The O.C., Punks!," August 5, 2003
by Daniel R. Coleridge
www.tvguide.com

TV Tome
www.tvtome.com

UnderGroundOnline
"Adam Brody," August 2003
by Eric S. Elkins
www.ugo.com

Variety.com
"FOX, McG Peeling O.C.," November 7, 2002
by Josef Adalian
www.variety.com

Variety.com
"Pilot Casting Hot, Heavy," March 12, 2003
by Josef Adalian
www.variety.com

Williamstown Theatre Festival
www.wtfestival.org

ym.com
"We're Obsessed: *The O.C.*," September 2003
by Sarah Tomczak & Briyah Paley
www.ym.com

Zap2it.com
"Piper Perabo and Mischa Barton Aren't *Lost & Delirious*—Just in the Film," July 20, 2001
by Mike Szymanski

Zap2it.com
"TV Gal Review: *The O.C.*," June 24, 2003
by Amy Amatangelo
www.zap2it.com

Zap2it.com
"*The O.C.*: New Zip Code for Teen Drama," August 2003
by John Crook
www.zap2it.com

TV Special

Orange County: American Hip Factory, VH1, 2002
Produced by Lucas Traub

INDEX